Two week loan
Benthyciad pythefnos

Please return on or before the due date to avoid overdue charges
*A wnewch chi ddychwelyd ar neu cyn y dyddiad a nodir ar eich llyfr os
gwelwch yn dda, er mwyn osgoi taliadau*

http://library.cardiff.ac.uk
http://llyfrgell.caerdydd.ac.uk

THUCYDIDES
AND THE POLITICS
OF BIPOLARITY

THUCYDIDES
AND THE POLITICS
OF BIPOLARITY

PETER J. FLIESS

LOUISIANA STATE UNIVERSITY PRESS

To Helen and Linda

COPYRIGHT © 1966
LOUISIANA STATE UNIVERSITY PRESS
LIBRARY OF CONGRESS CATALOG CARD NUMBER: 66-17215
MANUFACTURED IN THE UNITED STATES OF AMERICA BY
THE PARTHENON PRESS, NASHVILLE, TENNESSEE
DESIGN BY JULES B. MCKEE

THE absence of romance in my history will, I fear, detract somewhat from its interest; but if it be judged useful by those inquirers who desire an exact knowledge of the past as an aid to the interpretation of the future, which in the course of human things must resemble if it does not reflect it, I shall be content. In fine, I have written my work, not as an essay which is to win the applause of the moment, but as a possession for all time.

THUCYDIDES, 1. 22. 4.

SOURCES, however, especially such as come from the hand of great men, are inexhaustible, and everyone must re-read the works which have been exploited a thousand times, because they present a peculiar aspect, not only to every reader and every century, but also to every time of life. It may be, for instance, that there is in Thucydides a fact of capital importance which somebody will note in a hundred years' time.

Jakob Burckhardt, *Reflections on History*.

PREFACE

This book is a study of international politics before and during the Peloponnesian War. Its main purpose is to present systematically the essence of political relations between the Greek states as contained in the history of the period. We shall therefore be concerned with the political problems posed by the war and the events leading up to it. To extract systematic knowledge from a historical account is always hazardous and often frustrating. However, I judge it to be entirely compatible with Thucydides' intent. He was writing, he said, for the guidance of men of all times and in all places, on the assumption that recurrent elements were present in varying historical circumstances. This assumption was based on the conviction that man has a nature.

Any systematic presentation must necessarily cause trepidation. There invariably is a temptation to superimpose theoretical categories upon the subject. Yet unless we understand the past as it understood itself, historical study has little value. I have therefore endeavored—whether successfully or not the reader must judge—to let the categories emerge from the historical substance. The second hazard lies in distortion, which no systematization can avoid since it must separate phases of life that are united in actuality.

There has been a growing belief that valuable practical lessons can be learned from the study of political circumstances which, though remote in time, are not unlike those confronting the world today. It is for that reason that the great war between Athens and Sparta has received renewed attention in recent years among an audience that goes well beyond professional students of classics and ancient history. The period's characteristic distribution of effective international power between two superpowers bears a striking resemblance to the bipolarization of power which has occurred on a global scale since 1945 and which has relegated all nations other than the United States and the Soviet Union to a different and inferior status.

I do not propose to articulate the frequently obvious parallels. Historical analogies are invariably vague, and their pertinence to concrete situations is limited. Dramatic technological innovations like thermonuclear weapons and long-range missiles have profoundly affected contemporary political and social relationships, forcing us to discard time-honored rules and generalizations. In comparing the international situations then and now, it must be understood that analogous positions were occupied by Sparta and the United States, on the one hand, and by Athens and the Soviet Union, on the other. It is also necessary to remember the basic differences between the Athenian democracy of the fifth century B.C. and the American democracy of today. The internal structure of the representative libertarian democracy seems quite different from that of the ancient *direct* radical democracy. Further difficulties of analogy arise from the fact that the Greek struggle took place within the context of one civilization, whereas the bipolar struggle today is global. Another important difference is that the Hellenic world was as yet undisturbed by the religious schisms and the subsequent rise of political ideologies which have complicated the problems of the modern world. But if the relevance of the Hellenic case to the present is thereby limited, the absence of ideological complication makes the power issue appear in far greater clarity and thus greatly facilitates analysis.

Despite these limitations much common substance remains. The role played by human nature in the course of historical events continues to be a modern problem. If, then, something is to be learned from history about man's perennial problems and about the ways in which he has tried to cope with them, the job at hand is to distinguish between human and environmental factors, insofar as the interaction between man and his environment permits. This, it is hoped, will provide knowledge about political action which is pertinent to the analysis of contemporary events.

The lessons which Thucydides' *History of the Peloponnesian War* teaches are anything but obvious. They support neither an idealistic nor a consistently realistic position. Thucydides seems to accept the general thesis of the Athenian imperialists that they had no choice but to hold on to their empire; yet in specific instances he often seems to condemn their actions. To understand such apparent inconsistencies, one must remember that those engaged in the political struggle had to be prepared to act in accordance with certain necessities which were not of their making, even if such action did not conform to generally accepted moral standards. But that does not mean that the realist, acting as such necessities demand, is absolved from observing moral standards altogether. The need to exercise power, at times even unjust power, cannot justify its abuse. The ambivalence in Thucydides' drama arises from two sources: the political necessities inherent in the circumstances which man can neither harness nor evade, and man's ambitious and passionate nature, which prevents him from exercising such rational choices as are open to him. In analyzing the politics of the period an attempt must be made to disentangle proper from improper uses of power, to distinguish between the inherent necessities and the area of free choice retained by man.

The study of the period is rendered difficult by sizable lacunae in the history and by the uncertainty of our knowledge. Thucydides' work is the only comprehensive primary source in existence, and this necessarily raises the question of his reliability. Students have recently developed increasing misgivings about his trustworthiness and have questioned the accuracy of a good many aspects of his account as pragmatic history. It is of course not surprising that a writer of 2,500 years ago should be found wanting in terms of the critical standards developed by modern historical science. But must we conclude on the basis of occasional misjudgments and factual inaccuracies that his work as a whole is not sufficiently reliable to be useful as a key to the understanding of the period? In perusing the extensive scholarly debate that has ensued over his veracity, one is led to conclude that by and large he has come out well. His objectivity and accuracy concerning particular events and conditions has at times been successfully challenged. But his grasp and understanding of the basic issues and broad trends of his time have not been convincingly refuted. His main purpose was to lay bare the basic political forces at work, and he went about this task with extraordinary care and objectivity. In trying to present these basic political forces I have therefore felt justified in accepting Thucydides' work as trustworthy in its main lines.

A word should be said about the methodological relevance of the speeches with which his narrative is generously interspersed. It has long been a moot point whether they should be accepted as authentic records of what was actually said, or whether they must be considered free fabrications. Fortunately, Thucydides enlightens us regarding his method, the difficulties encountered, and the efforts made to overcome them. Some of the speeches, he alleges, he heard himself; others he obtained from diverse sources. The need to rely on his own memory and on the memory of others precluded literal reconstructions. But he made his speakers say what he thought they might have said in a given condition, "adhering as closely as possible to the general sense of what they really said." * The speeches, then, are not free inventions, but take into account the position in which the speakers found themselves. The speeches could not invariably remain free of Thucydides' own judgment, nor does he make any such claim. Most likely they are what he says they are; that is, at times they come close to what was said, at times they reveal the political problems of the moment and make the speaker say what, given his intelligence, psychology, and bias, he was likely to have said or thought under the circumstances. Evidently, then, the speeches vary in their methodological role; not all of them re-

* All citations to Thucydides are from the Crawley translation. The text used is H. Stuart Jones (Oxford: Clarendon Press, 1955).

flect equal degrees of authenticity, nor are all equally free of Thucydides' subjective evaluations. I am therefore inclined to accept the view of those scholars who regard them as presenting the essentials of a given situation and, consequently, as being useful sources for an understanding of the politics of the time.

For facts and interpretations which are not plain deductions from Thucydides I have relied on the standard histories. Among older works I have found the histories by Eduard Meyer and Georg Busolt particularly useful. Although gaps have been filled and interpretations refined by more recent scholarship, these older works continue to provide much valid information and many perceptive insights into the problems dealt with here. I should also mention the work of Wilhelm Roscher, *Leben, Werk und Zeitalter des Thukydides,* which was published in 1842 and which contains much that is of value for an understanding of the problems created by the power dualism.

A word of explanation should be added concerning some of the terms used. Relations between the Greek states are referred to as "international" for the simple reason that, like modern nation-states, they did not recognize a superior legal authority. As a result we find in ancient Greece a mass of mutually independent "sovereign" entities. Secondly, the term "Spartans" is used throughout, even though Thucydides usually speaks of "Lacedaemonians." The former term is used for the sake of simplicity and general familiarity, except for quotations and for instances where the technical distinction must be made between the citizens of Sparta and other residents of the city, the Lacedaemonians, not enjoying political privileges.

For the benefit of the reader who is not acquainted with the history of the period, the Prologue summarizes major events from the end of the Persian War through the Peloponnesian War.

I am grateful to Professor Hermann Strasburger for commenting on the project in its early stages. Moreover, I am indebted to Professors Sir Ronald Syme, Eric Voegelin, Martin Wight, William C. Havard, Jr., and James A. Steintrager, who have read the manuscript and made many helpful suggestions. I should also like to ex-

CONTENTS

THUCYDIDES
AND THE POLITICS
OF BIPOLARITY

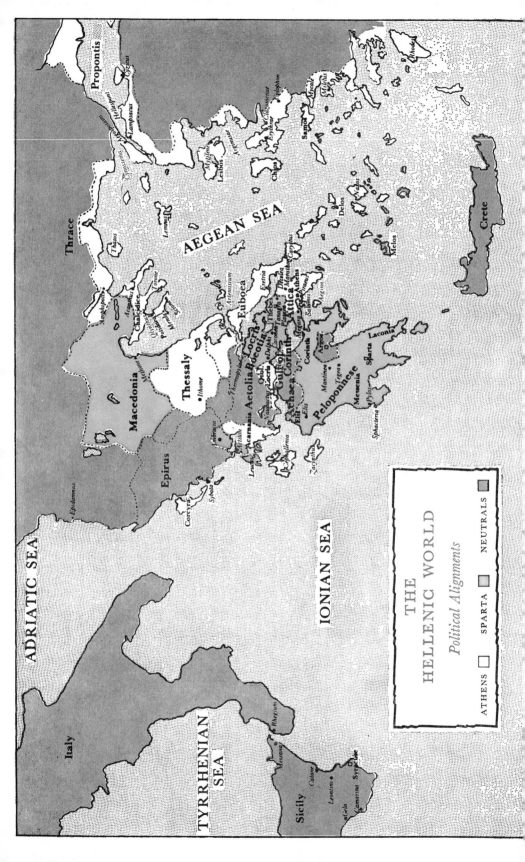

THE
HELLENIC WORLD
Political Alignments

ATHENS ☐ SPARTA ▨ NEUTRALS ▨

PROLOGUE

The origins of the problem with which this book is concerned reach back to the wars between the Greeks and the Persians at the beginning of the fifth century B.C. The consolidation and expansion of Persian power had brought the Greek cities on the Asia Minor coast under Persian rule. Around 500 B.C., when these Ionian Greeks revolted, economic, racial, and political ties caused them to look to their brethren on the Greek mainland for support. The response was disappointing. Only Athens and the city of Eretria on Euboea came to their aid, dispatching naval forces for their support. The intervention of mainland powers provided the Persian king with the rationale for attempting the conquest of Greece proper, which promised to be an easy undertaking because of the area's internal division.

In 490 a Persian fleet was sent out on a punitive expedition against the two mainland cities which had made bold to challenge the king's authority. This action was intended also to clear the road for the extension of Persian power over the entire Greek area. However, such plans were thwarted by the courageous resistance of the Athenians supported by their Plataean friends. The allies' daring action blocked the enemy's advance in the vicinity of Marathon, where the Persian fleet had landed, and forced his troops to sail homeward. Although Sparta was then the leading power in Greece, it had no part in the action. The forces which it dispatched in response to the Athenian appeal arrived too late to be of help.

When toward the end of the 480's there were signs that the Persians would launch a renewed attack against the Greek mainland, the Athenians became increasingly receptive to the plan of Themistocles, then their leading statesman, to build a powerful navy. As a result, Athens emerged as the leading naval power in Greece, fully matching Sparta's military might. Henceforward Greece was to have two leading powers.

In 480 Persian forces moved against Greece by land and by sea. This time Sparta, supported by Athens, took the lead in organizing a defensive league of all Greek cities determined to resist the attack. Greek forces, mostly Peloponnesians under the command of the Spartan king Leonidas, offered heroic resistance to Persian land forces at Thermopylae; although they could not hold their position against overwhelming Persian forces, they did succeed in delaying the Persian advance for several days. Since there was little chance of defeating Persian land forces, Athenian and Spartan leaders agreed that the crucial battles would have to be fought at sea. A decisive naval victory was won by the Aeginetans and the Athenians at Salamis. But the rout of their navy did not convince the Persians that their goals were unattainable. Continuing their advance by land, the Persians invaded Attica.

At this juncture signs of disharmony appeared among the Greek allies. Sparta was reluctant to do more than take a stand against the Persians at the Corinthian Isthmus. Only when the Athenians threatened to surrender to the enemy was Sparta at last persuaded to send troops into Central Greece. At Plataea the combined Greek forces, fighting with unprecedented unity and inspired by Spartan determination, finally dispersed the Persian army. Encouraged by their success, the Greeks now decided in favor of an offensive policy, pursuing the enemy fleet to Ionia where they won a decisive victory over Persian naval and land forces at the promontory of Mycale. This was the signal for the Ionian Greeks to defect from the Persians and seek admission to the Hellenic League for protection. When Sparta declined to accommodate the overseas Greeks, Athens interceded to secure the admission of Chios, Lesbos, and Samos and entered into alliance with several Ionian cities.

The years following the rout of the Persians were dominated by the growth of Athenian power. The foundation had been laid by Themistocles, who had early perceived the importance of a strong navy. The withdrawal of the Spartans from the continued war against the Persians further played into the hands of the Athenians, who were now assuming the part of protagonist of Hellenic freedom. To establish closer ties with the Ionians and the islands, in 478–77 they founded the Delian League, which would protect the outlying areas against renewed Persian attacks.

The persisting fears of the overseas Greeks, combined with Sparta's inability or unwillingness to assume the protectorate, virtually forced upon Athens the leadership of a large segment of the Greek world. Its naval supremacy immediately assured it of hegemony over the league, whose administrative center and treasury were to be located on the island of Delos. The larger cities, insofar as they were able, were to contribute ships to the common defense; the others were to make monetary contributions. The main beneficiary of the arrangement was Athens, which could further strengthen its naval supremacy through use of the payments made by the allies. Athens faithfully performed its part of the bargain by providing effective protection against Persian encroachments. Anticipating renewed attacks, the Athenians engaged Persian naval and land forces at the mouth of the Eurymedon River in Asia Minor about 467 and decisively defeated them.

The determined pursuit of the Persians had two effects: on one hand, it raised Athenian prestige throughout the Ionian world and brought more cities into the alliance; on the other hand, it encouraged defections from the league. Despite the protection which Athens was providing, many of the allies were not happy with this association. The obligations of membership were resented by many as excessively burdensome. Naxos had defected early, before the victory at the Eurymedon, and had been forcibly brought back into the fold. But once the Persian threat had been banished, the league seemed to have lost all justification, and a number of other allies refused continued compliance with the obligations of membership. The Athenians were especially embarrassed by the defection of the rich and powerful Thasos off the Thracian coast. The fact that the league had been concluded in perpetuity and was not formally linked to the presence of the Persian threat furnished them with the legal basis for coercive action. Severe punishment was meted out to defectors in the form of onerous tributes, leveling of fortifications, stationing of Attic garrisons, and allotting of land to Attic settlers.

With the elimination of the Persian threat and the tightening of Athenian control over the allies, the Spartans finally realized that their own position in Greece was threatened. In the years which followed, a number of external and internal events combined to lead Athens toward a consciously anti-Spartan policy. Although the pro-Spartan faction still controlled Athenian policy, the progressive democratization of Athens was causing a change in public opinion. In 464 when Sparta was hit by an earthquake, which invited a revolt of the *helots* and Messenian *perioeci,* Athens loyally dispatched troops to aid its old ally. However, when the Athenian troops made common cause with the rebels, the Spartans bluntly dismissed the Athenian forces. This insult provided the spark needed to displace the pro-Spartan with the anti-Spartan faction in Athens.

Athens, finding itself face-to-face with a weakened Sparta and an impotent Persia, decided to take the offensive against both simultaneously. Under the circumstances, it did not appear impossible to convert dominion over the Aegean Islands and Ionia to hegemony in Hellas. Sparta's difficulties in the Messenian war and in other parts of the Peloponnese had destroyed the myth of its invincibility. Moreover, the appeal of democratic ideas had enabled Athens to win allies in the Peloponnese and to gain the following of the Central Greek states; Athens thus appeared as a land power able to match Sparta. Sparta finally took up the challenge and met the Athenians in open battle at Tanagra. However, the Spartans did not exploit their victory politically. Athens soon restored its control over Boeotia, subjected Aegina, and launched successful forays into the Peloponnese. It also liberated Cyprus from Persian rule and seized bases in the East Mediterranean.

By 455 Athenian power had reached its high point. However, Athens overextended itself in pursuing the war against the Persians in Egypt. Superior Persian forces destroyed the Athenian expeditionary force, which had been dispatched to aid a local insurrection. The exposure of their domain to Persian attacks caused the Athenians to transfer the treasury of the Delian League to Athens and to abandon their two-front war. In 453 a five-year armistice was concluded with Sparta. Vis-à-vis Persia Athens was forced to relinquish its claims in Egypt, Cyprus, and the East Mediterranean. The so-called Peace of Callias was concluded in 449, leaving Athens in possession of its dominion over the Aegean and the Greek cities on the Asia Minor coast.

At the same time, Athens' problems on the mainland remained unresolved. The Central Greek states, Euboea, and Megara defected. In the thirty years' peace concluded with Sparta in 446–45 the Athenians had to renounce their influence in Central Greece and the Peloponnese. Athens now devoted its attention to consolidating its power over the Delian League. All resistance to Athenian authority was ruthlessly suppressed, and allied cities were converted into dependencies. In addition to considerations of prestige, the coercion of the allies had an eminently practical rationale. Their payment of tributes was an important source of revenue and helped finance the expensive public works projects demanded by the increasingly radical democracy.

The peace lasted approximately fifteen years. A number of incidents in the late 430's springing from the commercial and naval rivalry between Athens and Corinth (Sparta's ally) aroused suspicion in Sparta that the Athenians were resuming their old aggressiveness. Persistent Corinthian pressure and, even more, fear of Athens' seemingly irrepressible power drive motivated the Spartans in 431 to make war against the Athenians. With the outbreak of the war two great alliances, headed respectively by Athens and Sparta, were facing each other. Athens' allies were mostly overseas cities: the members of the Delian League including almost all the

Aegean Islands; in the West, Zacynthus and Corcyra in the Ionian Sea; and a number of colonies in Sicily and Italy. Its allies on land were limited to some of the Central Greek states. Sparta had allies in Central and Northern Greece, in addition to the Peloponnesians among whom only Argos and Achaea remained neutral.

The war resolved itself into three distinct phases: the so-called Archidamian War from 431 to 421, the Peace of Nicias from 421 to 414, and the Decelean War from 414 to 404. The early war years consisted mostly of annual Peloponnesian invasions of Attica aimed at the destruction of the enemy's economy. Athens in turn tried to strike at the Peloponnesian economy by blockading the Peloponnese. In spite of their initial advantage the Athenians suffered an early setback when the plague broke out in the second year of the war, demoralizing the people and claiming the life of Pericles, their leader. Athens recovered from the disaster, but leadership passed into the hands of demagogues lacking in vision and dedication. Nevertheless by 425 the war had again turned in favor of the Athenians. However, the fortunes were soon to change. Spartan forces under Brasidas advanced toward Chalcidice and Thrace and persuaded Athens' allies to defect. Athenian attempts to reconquer them were unsuccessful.

An important incision in the war came with the battle of Amphipolis in 422 which claimed the lives of Brasidas and the Athenian leader Cleon, who had been the driving forces of the war factions on both sides. The death of the two leaders cleared the way for negotiations. Both in Athens and Sparta the peace factions were now gaining, and in 421 a fifty years' peace was concluded. Under its provisions Spartan prisoners were to be returned, and all the cities of the Delian League which had defected to the Spartans were to be restored to Athens. But both sides fell short of fulfilling the obligations of the peace. In particular, the refusal of some of Sparta's allies to accept the treaty prevented Sparta from living up to its commitments, and this in turn led to retaliations by Athens. Deserted by many of its allies Sparta entered into a fifty years' alliance with Athens. The treaty in effect was a mutual assistance pact in the event of invasion, combined with an agreement not to make a separate peace. The conclusion of the alliance, which had all the appearance of a colossal betrayal, aroused widespread suspicion among the Peloponnesians. Elis and Mantinea revolted and entered into alliance with Sparta's traditional enemy Argos. For several years Sparta's hegemony in the Peloponnese was in question, and it was restored only after Spartan forces had defeated the Argives in the battle of Mantinea in 418. In Athens the tenuous peace produced considerable discontent. With the passage of time, the horrors of war had been forgotten, and the policy of Nicias' moderate faction was being challenged by the radical faction led by Alcibiades. The latter's success in conquering the neutral island of Melos, a Spartan colony which had resisted integration into the Athenian empire, brought his faction into the lead.

The turning point in the war came with the adoption of Alcibiades' ambitious plan to conquer Sicily. If successful, the plan would enable the Athenians to become the masters of all of Greece and would eventually make possible a showdown with Carthage. The objections of Alcibiades' political rival Nicias, who had warned against the inordinate risks involved in so daring an expedition, were overruled. The venture got off to a bad start. Before the expedition departed, pranksters committed an act of sacrilege by mutilating statues of Hermes in the streets. Excitement was widespread inasmuch as this was considered a bad omen for the impending expedition. Alcibiades, whose name had been mentioned as a possible instigator of the prank, urged that the matter be cleared up. It was initially decided to postpone the investigation until after the expedition had completed its mission. However, growing popular excitement brooked no delay, and Alcibiades was recalled to stand trial soon after the expedition had gone to sea. Doubtful that he would be dealt with fairly, he escaped to Sparta.

Alcibiades' counsels fully awakened the Spartans to the magnitude of the Athenian threat. The Spartans could ill-afford to close their minds to the information disclosed by the mastermind of Athenian policy; they heeded his advice by placing Gylippus, one of the best Spartan generals, in command of the defense of Syracuse. Soon after Gylippus assumed command, the fortunes of war turned against the Athenian expeditionary force, and it was completely destroyed in the summer of 413. The disaster was largely the result of irresolute leadership. With the recall of Alcibiades, Nicias had remained in command; Nicias, who was handicapped by his congenital caution and fear of the vagaries of the Athenian masses, had been opposed to the expedition from the outset. Athenian strategy was further encumbered by disagreements between Nicias and his fellow general, Demosthenes.

The annihilation of the Athenian force in Sicily was the decisive event of the war. The weakness of Athens encouraged many of its allies to defect. It also induced the Persians to give active support to Sparta and to violate the Peace of Callias by collecting tribute from the Ionian Greeks. In the midst of the Sicilian War in 414 hostilities between Athens and Sparta were resumed. On the advice of Alcibiades, the Spartans occupied a fortified position at Decelea in Attica, from which they devastated the Attic countryside and imposed a land blockade on Athens.

Military reverses and the deterioration of finances led to the collapse of democracy in Athens. In 411 the democratic government was forced to give way to the oligarchic rule of the Four Hundred, which in turn was displaced within a few months by the government of the Five Thousand well-to-do citizens. This moderate government, which remained in power for eight months, could not reverse the unfavorable situation in which Athens found itself as a result of the setbacks suffered. In their distress the Athenians recalled Alcibiades, who defended the empire from Samos, defeated the Spartans in a naval battle at Cyzicus in 410, and reconquered some of the outlying areas that had been lost. He was entrusted with the supreme command of Athenian land and naval forces.

By this time Athens was too exhausted even for Alcibiades' genius to save the day. With Persian aid the Spartans had built a navy, and they had found a leader—Lysander—who was fully Alcibiades' match. Lysander defeated the Athenians in a naval battle at Notium in 407, following which Alcibiades was stripped of his command. But Athens once again staged a comeback and assembled a new fleet with the help of its faithful ally Samos, which dealt a crushing blow to the Spartans at Arginusae. A peace offer made by the Spartans was rejected because the Athenians refused to settle for less than the evacuation of all cities that had belonged to their empire. Pressed by the Spartans from Decelea and cut off from their supply line, the Athenians tried to reopen passage at the Hellespont. However, at Aegospotami almost the entire Athenian fleet was captured, and Athens' fate was sealed.

The Athenians were forced to surrender themselves to the mercy of the Spartans. Although the terms were severe, Sparta dealt more mercifully with the population of the defeated city than might have been expected in view of the many atrocities they had committed during the war. Sparta allegedly was not interested in destroying the city to which the cause of Hellenic freedom had owed so much during the Persian War.

chapter 1

BIPOLARITY
AND THIRD POWERS

BIPOLARITY AS AN OBJECTIVE CONDITION

Thucydides intended his *History of the Peloponnesian War* to be more than a chronological account of events. He hoped that there would emerge from the unique occurrences he described a knowledge of universal truths about man which would make the study of these events a rewarding experience for posterity. The work therefore requires of the reader a desire to study the effect of human nature upon the thoughts and impulses of men. Thucydides' hopes have been realized to a high degree. Although the lessons he was trying to teach have not been the subject of continuous interest, his work has recurrently commanded the attention of both statesmen and students and has provided in periods of ferment a virtually inexhaustible fund of practical knowledge concerning diplomacy, war, revolution, and other matters relevant to politics. No doubt he would have been gratified by the renewed interest which his work has aroused in recent years.

For all the seriousness with which his *History* has been studied, scant justice has been done to the implications of the bipolarization of power. To be sure, Thucydides' basic concern with the concentration of total destructive force in the hands of only two "superpowers" and its more or less equal division between them has been widely acknowledged. What has been neglected is the

13

limitations which that power constellation has steadily imposed on the freedom of action of states. The extraordinary restriction of political choices alone seems sufficient reason to make a sharp distinction between the bipolar and the more common diversified power constellations. What was of particular consequence was the fact that the combined or individual striking forces of the superpowers could not be matched by any other state or combination of states; thus exclusive control of international politics was concentrated in two powers solely responsible for preserving the peace or making war.

Bipolarity described

So stated, of course, bipolarity is unduly simplified. Few situations are simple and unequivocal, and it is frequently difficult to say just when a given political type has emerged sufficiently to be relevant to analysis. Even where political action has come ultimately to depend on the competitive struggle between two blocs, powers, empires, or alliances, enough contrary tendencies remain to obscure the issue. Complete internal unity of the two camps or the integration of all third powers cannot reasonably be expected under the most favorable conditions. We would also search in vain for identical forms of internal organization in the two blocs facing each other in the Peloponnesian War. Appreciable differences can be observed not only in formal structure but also in the substantive relations between the leading and the dependent states. We are told of a strict, even tyrannical, rule by the Athenians over an empire of satellites. By contrast, Thucydides is more charitable toward the Spartan bloc, to which he refers in such noncommittal terms as "the Lacedaemonians and their allies."

If the lines are thus blurred, it is necessary first of all to ascertain whether we are actually face to face with a bipolar constellation. A problem that immediately comes to mind is the role played by neighboring non-Greek peoples. Did they remain aloof from the intra-Hellenic struggle for supremacy? And if they did become involved, were they mere appendages to the Hellenic balance of power, or did they constitute an independent third force actively involved in a triangular conflict? The degree of influence exercised by the Persians is of particular interest. No doubt the dramatic defeat they had suffered at the hands of the Greeks on land and on the sea at Salamis, Plataea, and Mycale forced them to abandon, at least temporarily, their plans for bringing Greece under their control. But this was not in itself sufficient reason to consider their expulsion from Europe as final. If they could not control the Greeks directly, they might still try to bring some influence to bear on their politics. It must also be remembered that in historical perspective the period is notable above all for the prolonged and embittered contest between the Persian empire and the West, which provides the broader frame for interludes of a parochial nature.[1] In that contest the Greeks were to play an important part; however, their contribution had to remain limited in time and scope partly because of the area's small size, but more importantly because of its debilitating political fragmentation.

If from a long-range point of view Greece then seems little more than a frontier of the Persian empire, the disparate Greek *polis* world nevertheless succeeded, during the interval between the rout of the Persian forces in 480–79 and Athens' defeat at Aegospotami in 405, in raising itself above the level of a mere appendage to the powerful Persian realm. During that period the Greeks were masters in their own house, and they made history in their own right by holding the Asian onslaught at bay. Only during the later phases of the Peloponnesian War did the Persians enter into Hellenic politics again by attempting to widen the political split of Hellas in order to devitalize the region as far as possible.

Between the rout of the Persians and their renewed involvement in Greek politics, there existed a coherent balance-of-power system centered in Hellas with the barbarian areas as its fringe. The Peloponnesian War in particular was entirely Hellenic. The stakes for which it was fought were clearly related to the distribution of power in Hellas proper, with little direct bearing on the showdown between East and West. When the Spartans finally decided to go to war, they did so out of fear for their independence should

Athens' growing power be permitted to throw the Hellenic balance out of gear.[2]

Influence of barbarians

All this is not to say that the Greeks had isolated themselves from the neighboring barbarian world or were consciously trying to do so. In fact, both sides sooner or later tried their best to enlist the support of their non-Greek neighbors and to solicit them as allies against other Greeks. Throughout the war, and especially in its later phases, rapprochements and even connivances between Greeks and Persians were common. Such collaboration may seem strange in view of the Greeks' highly developed sense of forming an exclusive ethnic community, a propensity which was strong enough to provoke repeated outbursts of Hellenic nationalism at times overriding considerations of strategic advantage even in moments of greatest need. A good example is furnished by the Spartan renunciation of treaties which had acknowledged the Persian king's claim to all the country formerly ruled by himself or his ancestors including the islands, Thessaly, Locris, and "everything as far as Boeotia." [3] If the price to be paid was a sell-out of Greeks, the Spartans were willing to forego Persian aid no matter how urgently it was needed. And, toward the end of the war, the Spartan admiral Callicratidas, angered by discourteous treatment from the Persians, pleaded for a common Greek front against the barbarians; if Xenophon is to be trusted, Callicratidas also asked for a reconciliation between the Spartans and the Athenians.[4]

Despite the presence of nationalistic sentiments, Greek collaboration with barbarians was quite common when expedient. Thucydides reports that shortly after the repulsion of the Persians, the Spartan regent Pausanias, conspired with the former enemy, with whose aid he hoped to make himself the ruler of Hellas.[5] Even more illuminating is an offer made by the great patriot Themistocles to assist the Persian king in the subjugation of Hellas. The offer was extended while Themistocles was in exile from his native land after the Persian War.[6] The importance of episodes of this kind should not be overestimated. They were isolated instances and very likely no more than attempts to satisfy personal ambition. But even when seen in the proper light, they do suggest the tenuousness of Hellenic nationalism. It is not surprising therefore that under the impact of a war of such ferocity as the Peloponnesian War, the customary contempt for barbarians should have disappeared almost entirely. Pride and prejudice had to give way before the great fears inspired by the possibility that one of the contestants in the bipolar struggle for supremacy might emerge as unlimited ruler.

We should thus be prepared to find the barbarians included in the estimates of both belligerents.[7] Although no barbarian tribe was too lowly to be ignored, the powerful Persians understandably were the main non-Greek subjects of solicitation. The Athenians, it is true, initially showed some reluctance toward such undignified friendships. But the conservative Spartans cavalierly cast aside traditional prejudices, giving top priority to strategic needs. It became increasingly apparent to them, as the war progressed, that decisive victories could be scored only with the aid of a fleet capable of matching the striking power of the Athenian navy. But it was equally obvious that they could not build a navy of such proportions without outside financial support. Since expectations of aid from their Dorian brethren in Sicily and Italy had failed to materialize, the Persian king remained as their only hope. But even so, in the initial phase of the war when the need for support was not so overwhelming, the Spartans were wary enough of such ties to refuse the king's requirement that the Greek cities in Asia be returned to him. In making such a concession Sparta would have seriously impaired the effectiveness of its professed policy of liberating the cities that were chafing under Athenian rule.[8] But later, when the war had become increasingly intense and desperate, even such reservations were brushed aside; eventually no price seemed too high for Persian financial and naval aid.

The Athenians, who initially had reason to view their prospects optimistically, persisted somewhat longer in their snobbishness toward the barbarians; but the prolonged and uncommonly ferocious war soon forced them to adopt a humbler attitude and to seek barbarian support wherever possible. Although no appeal seems to have been made to the Persians before 424, the Athenians had all along maintained close relations with the Thracians and the Macedonians.[9] At a later point the Athenian expedition to Sicily, the greatest single venture of the war, was clearly premised on the expectation of barbarian contributions.[10] Eventually the Athenians even looked to the hated Persians as potential donors of financial and military aid.[11] The net effect of the growing inclination of both sides to court the great king's favor [12] was that the ruler of the barbarian empire was exalted to a pivotal position in Hellenic politics. The pleas of both belligerents became increasingly intense as the war dragged on and their stamina decreased.

The barbarians' response to such appeals was not uniformly enthusiastic. The policy of the Persians in particular wavered considerably. Their rout at Salamis and the internal weakness of the empire forced them to stand aloof of Greek politics for the time being. But even so, no Iron Curtain was rung down between Greece and Persia, and Persian interest in the Greek settlements in Asia Minor and in the Aegean islands remained lively. However, for a long time Persian involvement in Greek affairs was of little significance. After the conclusion of the Peace of Callias with the Athenians in 449, there actually was little Persian interference in Greek affairs, and this did not change when the Peloponnesian War broke out. Not until the seventh year of the war did the Spartans receive a mildly encouraging response to their pleas, and even then no concrete promise was held out for the future.[13] However, during the last phase of the war, the so-called Decelean War, the role of the Persians changed drastically. Although internal difficulties long continued to prevent them from openly entering the arena of the Hellenic war, they responded to the Spartans' pleas for help when the concessions which they had demanded were finally made. Eventually the Persians concluded several treaties of alliance with the Peloponnesians in which they undertook to fight the war jointly and not to make a separate peace.[14]

The conclusion of the treaties undoubtedly was a major triumph for the Peloponnesian cause. However, the immediate practical effect must not be overestimated. Even after such far-reaching commitments had been assumed, Persian support remained unreliable. The Persians showed little enthusiasm in giving aid, nor did they betray an unequivocal hostility toward the common enemy.[15] As for the Athenians, they were far from willing to close the door to an eventual rapprochement with Persia. Severe setbacks as well as the partiality of the Persians to the Peloponnesian side had eventually forced the Athenians to take a pessimistic view of their prospects and ultimately to seek negotiations with the despised barbarians.[16] Their anxiety even made them recall the traitor Alcibiades from exile because of his presumed friendship with Tissaphernes, the Persian satrap; through this friendship they hoped to secure Persian aid.[17] Such hopes were not entirely without foundation. Tissaphernes had been receptive to Alcibiades' advice "not to put the power by land and by sea into the same hands" and was prepared to play a dual game.[18] It was only when the final decision could be postponed no longer that the king brought Tissaphernes' duplicity to a halt and promised his full support to the Peloponnesians. The king's pro-Spartan sympathies were entirely realistic. The Peloponnesians, if victorious, could reasonably be expected to withdraw into their isolationist shell. By contrast, a victorious Athens would press its claims to hegemony over Ionia and thus thwart the goals of Persian policy.[19]

Other barbarians, such as the Thracians and Macedonians, were also drawn into the Hellenic contest at times;[20] but their participation was haphazard and marginal since none had a clearly formulated policy concerning its relations with the Greeks.

What effect did the barbarian participation have upon the outcome of the war? Can it still be said that the power constellation of the period was bipolar in character? For purposes of such an assessment the influence of barbarians other than Persians can be dismissed as insignificant. Although eventually the Macedonian invasion was to be politically fateful for Hellas, at the time of the Peloponnesian War their participation was of little consequence. More problematical are the circumstances of the Sicilian expedition. Although the part played by the Sicilians is undeniably great, a good case can be made for considering Sicily part and parcel of the Greek power system. Ethnically the Sicilians were Greeks, and political as well as commercial ties closely linked them to the area of their origin. They had long been engaged in political and commercial rivalry with Athens, while maintaining friendly relations with the Peloponnesians almost from the beginning of the war. Sicily can therefore fairly be regarded as a geographic extension of Greece, which like all Greek areas was drawn into the contest between the two leading cities.

Persian participation poses a more serious problem because of its decisive effect upon the outcome of the war. The crucial importance of the Persian intervention is a matter of record. But it is also clear that almost to the end they were reluctant to commit themselves unconditionally to the Peloponnesian cause. Had they wanted to participate in the Greek conflict in earnest, they would probably have proceeded differently. In alliance with Greeks they might have fought for tangible aims of their own and destroyed the Hellenic balance by helping one side or the other to win a speedy victory; but Persian participation was limited and haphazard during most of the war. Hardly any Persian troops were involved in military operations, and commitments for monetary aid were invariably unreliable.[21] All the evidence tends to confirm that Persian interventions, both in design and effect, were to intensify and perpetuate the dualism of power in Hellas, with the apparent purpose of keeping the war going as long as possible.

Whatever the reasons, Persia did not enter the conflict in earnest. Only toward the very end did King Darius resolutely and systematically support the Spartan cause. The war thus was and remained Hellenic. The political dualism between Athens and Sparta had been its cause and remained the principal issue until the ultimate defeat of Athens.

The balance in Hellas

That the Hellenic balance-of-power system was relatively independent of external influences, we cannot therefore doubt. What
remains to be examined is the pattern of power within that system. Just when the division of Hellas into two power spheres
entered into the common awareness of the period, it is difficult to
say. The utmost that can be said is that the new alignment probably was an established fact as early as 470 (when Athens made
it clear that any secession from the Delian League would be
dealt with severely) and was generally recognized by 460. However, the new distribution of power was formally recognized
only with the settlement of 446, through which the Athenians
and the Spartans attempted to define and stabilize the bipolar
balance. When war finally broke out, the central issue was
the clash of two imperial blocs provoked by the rapid growth of
Athenian power which threatened to upset the precarious balance.[22]

Although the involvement of other Greek states and substantial
parts of the adjacent barbarian world was bound to infuse particularistic interests into the conflict, the great issues were between
Athens and Sparta.[23] By the time the war got underway the
unique position of the two leading powers wholly dominated the
political and military picture. There was hardly any state that
could make policy without reference to them and without making
sure that it could count on the support of one in case of conflict
with the other. A case in point is the defection of Thasos in 464
from the Athenian alliance, which was accompanied by an appeal
for Spartan aid.[24] And those who seceded from the Peloponnesian
alliance would attach themselves to Athens as a matter of course.
This was true in 455 of states that had been defeated or rebuffed
by the Spartans;[25] and it had been true in 478 of those who, when
oppressed in Sparta's name by the corrupt Pausanias, implored
Athens to assume their hegemony.[26] But perhaps the bipolar
pattern of politics is most clearly reflected in the restrictions which
circumstances imposed upon the main antagonists themselves, who
were no longer free in defining the roles they were to play in the

contest. Their uneven political and military development, as will be shown in the following chapter, destined the one to pursue an expansionist policy and the other to commit itself to defense of the status quo. Sparta's role as liberator of Hellas was therefore less an expression of intrinsic virtue than the logical consequence of its defensive position.

The impact of the war was felt everywhere, and few decisions of any importance were made which were not dictated by the exigencies of bipolar politics. It will not be necessary to present here an exhaustive catalogue of examples to demonstrate the extent to which the entire area was caught up in the gigantic contest. A few examples gleaned from the pages of Thucydides will suffice as illustrations. The news of the débâcle in Sicily threw not only Athens but the entire Hellenic world into a state of abjection.[27] When early in the war the Athenians expelled their unfriendly Aeginetan neighbors from their homes for reasons of security, it was a matter of course that the Peloponnesians should welcome the Aeginetans as friends and give them new homes. There was no other visible reason for such hospitality than their quarrel with the Athenians.[28] Nor was it accidental that Sparta, upon expiry of its thirty years' truce with Argos in 421, simply assumed that failure to renew it would drive its neighbor into alliance with Athens. Apparently little thought was given to the possibility that Argos might pursue an independent policy.[29] Again, the exigencies of bipolarism were largely responsible for disturbing the Peace of Nicias, which separated the first and second phases of the war, since neither of the leading powers was able to cast off the role that had fallen to it in the bipolar contest.

BIPOLARITY AS A PSYCHOLOGICAL REALITY

In this new world where established principles had lost both their rationale and their utility, the constant temptation to abandon traditional values could not fail to bring on a weakening of organic cohesion. Loyalties based on a community of tradition and kinship were displaced by considerations of power.[30] The dissolution of traditional bonds is particularly apparent in the case of those morally and politically aligned with Sparta, who were committing themselves with an uncommon single-mindedness to the destruction of their political opponent.[31] Even implacable tribal antagonisms were overcome in order to present a united front against the Athenian conquerors. A clear example is Sicily, where the Syracusan leader Hermocrates extolled the fatherland as a geographic rather than an ethnic concept and in the name of freedom appealed especially to the Ionian component of the Sicilian population: "Nor should any one imagine that the Dorians only are enemies of Athens, while the Chalcidian race is secured by its Ionian blood; the attack in question is not inspired by hatred of one of two nationalities, but by a desire for the good things in Sicily, the common property of us all." [32] Further examples could be cited, especially in relation to the balance-of-power and the alliance systems. However, a detailed treatment of these and related issues will be reserved for later chapters.

Despite such evident basic changes in political values, the new distribution of power did not find immediate expression in contemporary thought. The *polis* had in fact remained the highest focus of allegiance of its citizens, and no political organization of a higher order had as yet superseded it. Such discrepancies between political values and political fact are not uncommon; the emotional attachments of a people frequently are dangerously out of tune with the world of facts. Yet the demands of practical necessity were too overwhelming to be resisted. The exaggerated adulation of the *polis* was a luxury which only the people of the most powerful city-states could afford. The inhabitants of the less powerful cities were continually forced to disregard their most cherished beliefs and throw in their lot with Athens or Sparta, even at the expense of their city's independence. Circumstances had in most cases reduced the coveted autonomy and international equality of the *polis* to a mere illusion, and any attempt to use this distorted image of reality as a basis for further political action was to build upon sand.

Thucydides' view

But is there any evidence that the predicament which the bipolarization of power created had entered into the political consciousness of the period? In the absence of other equally reliable sources we must here be content with the evidence provided by Thucydides' own understanding and the opinions he attributed to his contemporaries. There can be no doubt that he was aware of the problem and judged it to be of prime importance. The very choice of his subject as stated in the opening sentence of his work makes this clear. He did not set out merely to describe in chronological order a series of battles and intermittent diplomatic negotiations. His avowed purpose was to write the history of the "war between the Peloponnesians and Athenians." Cutting through the crust of external appearances, he attempted to lay bare the real issue connecting particular events. Undeterred by pretenses he probed the reasons for the war until he had traced its ultimate cause to the Spartans' fear of the growth of Athenian power,[33] a power which could no longer be contained unless Sparta secured military supremacy. The tale might have been told differently—in terms of the intrinsic interest in military operations, the failure of imperialism, the ethical dilemma of power politics, ethnic conflicts, and so on. Although none of these subjects are neglected, the organizing principle which gives unity to the seeming chaos of events in the *History* was provided by the Atheno-Spartan dualism.

Thucydides' choice of the dates 431 and 404 to signify the beginning and the end of the war is particularly revealing. There was no immediately apparent reason for grouping the Archidamian War from 431 to 421, the Peace of Nicias from 421 to 414, and the Decelean War from 414 to 404 together into one unit. The need for placing his incisions where he did, that is, at 431 and 404, becomes apparent only in the light of the ultimate cause which he had discovered. It was entirely possible to date the beginning of the war much earlier, so as to include the period frequently referred to as the First Peloponnesian War (464–446). It may seem equally debatable whether the war was actually terminated with the defeat of Athens at Aegospotami. The story could easily be carried beyond the year 404, as Xenophon and Theopompus did. To be sure, Thucydides did not survive the collapse of Athens long enough to see that it failed to bring about the pacification of Hellas. However, his profound knowledge of Greek politics might have led him to be more tentative concerning the duration of the war than he was. Regardless of when and in what order he wrote his *History* (a question that has remained the object of scholarly controversy), he could be so certain concerning the end of the war only because he had recognized the political dualism as its ultimate cause. It might of course be objected that the military clashes between 464 and 446, like those of the Peloponnesian War, resulted from the rivalry of the two hegemonial cities. However, there was a difference between the earlier period when the bipolar balance was still inchoate and the later chain of events after 431 when the balance was fully developed. The date designating the termination of the war can be similarly explained since the conflict sparked by the bipolarization of power had been resolved with the defeat of one of the polar powers.

The importance which Thucydides attached to the Spartan-Athenian dualism as the driving force of the war is perhaps most clearly reflected by his assertion that this was the greatest convulsion ever experienced by mankind.[34] Qualitatively the war was unique for producing universal repercussions. Unlike most wars it transcended the usual bounds of an armed international conflict, in that it assumed the form and proportions of internecine war. In arousing passions of the greatest intensity and subverting the Greek *ethos*, it represented the "breakdown of the fabric of Greek society."[35] Quantitatively, too, the war was of singular magnitude. Preparations on both sides reached extraordinary heights and the fighting, with few exceptions, encompassed the entire Hellenic world.[36] Although some degree of neutrality was tolerated initially, no Greek could remain emotionally indifferent as all Hellas watched with tension and anxiety the impending conflict between the two leading cities.[37] The awareness that the balance of power of the entire area would depend on the outcome of the war was enough to alert the people to its great significance.

In addition to direct statements, Thucydides provides many clues which indicate what he considered to be the overriding issue. A case in point is his insertion of a description of the fifty-year period preceding the outbreak of the war, which is remarkable in view of his usual conciseness.[38] His purpose in explaining the growth of the Athenian empire [39] was closely linked to the predicament confronting the Hellenic world. All issues and aspirations were overshadowed by a mutual, unrelenting fear which had resulted from the disappearance of third powers of any consequence. The excursus on the fifty-year period was intended to explain the origins of that predicament.

Other examples may be cited. Mention is made of the split between Athens and Sparta, which occurred during the Persian War and produced a divided hegemony.[40] An explicit acknowledgment of the bipolarization of power is put in Pericles' mouth when he informed his Athenian listeners that the hegemony of Hellas was divided between the hegemony on land, which was Sparta's, and the maritime hegemony of Athens.[41] Following the same line of reasoning both sides expressed the fear that, in the absence of a balancing power, their defected allies would have no choice but to join the enemy.[42] Awareness of the issue again appears in the speech of the Corinthians in Sparta, preceding the outbreak of the war, which states that the Athenians were a match for the entire Peloponnesian Confederacy.[43] In the same vein was the Athenian prediction that in the absence of a balancer Sparta's popularity would quickly vanish if Athens were defeated,[44] since this would leave Sparta unrestrained by any external forces.

The general Hellenic view

Thucydides' own view that the bipolarization of power was the basic issue in the war thus seems clear. But he also leaves us with the impression that his contemporaries were equally aware of the tragic predicament this distribution of power had created. In view of his own passion for accuracy and the tenor of other literary works of the period, it is more than likely that contemporary political thought was cast in the categories of the Atheno-Spartan dualism.[45] Comparisons and contrasts of the national character of the hegemonial cities were standard subjects of political speeches and debates. Further support is provided by the military and political situation. The so-called First Peloponnesian War had brought the conflict between Athens and Sparta into the open, and so did the settlement of 446 which concluded it.

All this is taken for granted by Thucydides when he reports the candid Spartan acknowledgment, after their defeat at Pylos in 425, that "the rest of Hellas will remain in respectful inferiority before its heads."[46] His observation that all Hellas had been aroused by the disaster which Athenian forces in Sicily suffered[47] cannot have been pure fabrication. Even if it be granted that a calamitous defeat of a major power would ordinarily reverberate throughout the entire balance-of-power system of which it is a member, the great fermentation which Thucydides attributes to the Athenian rout does evoke surprise. In view of Thucydides' well-known aversion to exaggeration, we may accept the fact that everybody actually was deeply affected by the consequences. This profound concern can be explained only in terms of the consequences which they expected the disaster to have for all of them, and this expectation points to their consciousness of the facts at issue. There could be little doubt that disaster befalling one of the leading cities would not merely cause a shift in the existing balance but totally destroy it. The uncertainty that would follow from the rule of one virtually unrestrained leader plausibly explains their alarm.

chapter 2

PRELUDE
TO BIPOLARITY

FORMATION OF A UNITED FRONT

To understand the origins of the bipolar balance of power, the fifty-year period preceding the outbreak of the Peloponnesian War must be examined more closely; the events of this period account for the displacement of Sparta's Hellenic leadership by a dual hegemony. Unfortunately the paucity of contemporary sources seriously restricts our knowledge. Aside from Thucydides' brief digression,[1] only minor fragments of other accounts have been preserved. Reports by later writers, such as Plutarch and Diodorus Siculus, do not measure up to Thucydides' standards of accuracy or to the depth of his insights. We have therefore little more to go on than the evidence of Thucydides' chapters, which merely outline political developments and are not overly detailed. However, the absence of full particulars does not prevent us from exploring the problem which concerns us here, that is, the rise of a second *hegemon* in Greece.

A brief examination of the historical context in which this strange development took place may shed some light on the matter. The Hellenic area had traditionally been divided into numerous mutually independent city-states, among which Sparta had for some time occupied a leading position. The beginnings of Sparta's superior position can be traced back to the end of the sixth century when the Peloponnesian Confederacy came into being through alliances concluded with most of the Peloponnesian states.[2] Though regional in scope, the organization rested more on political than on geographic factors.[3] It was above all a league of oligarchies, compelled by their inferior military power to rally around a protector who would coordinate their foreign affairs.[4] Its remarkable durability no doubt is a measure of the wise restraint which marked Sparta's leadership. The latter's constant readiness to provide military aid where demanded, combined with a meticulous respect for the members' autonomy,[5] made the obligations of membership appear small payment for the advantages which it implied.

Sparta's leadership was further strengthened and extended when Persian armies attacked the Greek mainland. To be sure, its influence and authority had transcended the confines of the Peloponnese even before then. Sparta had long played a dominant role in such activities of all-Greek interest as the olympiades and religious and cultural pursuits in general. But such cult functions, although they called forth a measure of Panhellenic cooperation, had more symbolic than practical political significance. However, in time Sparta was to exploit its great prestige and military power for political ends, transforming its perfunctory primacy into a more tangible political role when it undertook to stamp out the remaining tyrannies in Hellas. It was therefore only natural that when the Persian threat arose, all Hellas should have looked to Sparta for leadership. Athens, which was the chief target of the first Persian expeditionary force of 490, was no exception since there was no other Greek power of similar strength it could turn to for help.[6] When ten years later the Persians resumed their attack, the Greek states that were prepared to resist the invaders once again rallied around Sparta, even though it had been the Athenians who turned the enemy back at Marathon on the first try. In view of its military supremacy, its leadership of the Peloponnesian League, and its traditional opposition to Persia, Sparta naturally appeared as the appropriate rallying point for a concerted defense effort.[7]

Sparta slowly assumed the responsibility which its leading position had thrust upon it. The magnitude of the Persian threat required above all a concentration of military resources, and Sparta did proceed to take the initiative in forming a league of Greek states, which it hoped would be Panhellenic in its membership. Granting the command of the allied forces to Sparta was not a matter of course, perhaps, but it is understandable enough that the members should thus have expressed their confidence in a leader who seemed to be discharging his obligations effectively.[8] When the victory at Plataea seemed to have averted the Persian menace for the time being, the allies proceeded to transform the temporary defensive alliance into a permanent organization—with Sparta as its *hegemon*—for the continued pursuit of the war against Persia.[9] Although the defense of Greece was off to a promising start, much remained to be done. Many states were still under Persian rule, and it was necessary to maintain a ready defensive apparatus to secure the gains that had been made and to resist possible future Persian attacks.

The political implications of the unprecedented degree of Hellenic solidarity which the formation of the league reflected are hard to overrate. Although Panhellenic sentiments and cult practices reached far back, Hellas had never been more than a geographic and perhaps a cultural concept. No common political action appears to have taken place before the Trojan War,[10] and not even that traumatic experience could appreciably reduce the area's political diversity. However, in the face of the Persian attack Hellas succeeded in transcending its geographic meaning by developing a genuine sense of political unity. Interestingly enough, the Ionians were looking upon their revolt against the Persian king as a war involving all-Greek concerns, and in 499 they turned for help to Sparta and Athens, their brethren on the Greek mainland.[11] What is more, their appeals were made in terms of an ethnic community which they allegedly shared with the mainland Greeks.[12] But even some forty years earlier the Spartans had already put the Persian king on notice that they would not tolerate encroachments upon any Greek city.[13] Although Sparta did not extend tangible aid as long as hostilities between Greeks and Persians were confined to Asia Minor, it actually managed to bring the Peloponnesian League into alliance with the Greek states abroad when the Greek mainland was threatened. Evidently, most Greeks were sufficiently aroused by the barbarian threat against their freedom and way of life to abandon temporarily their conflicts and unite for common action.

By far the most promising development in the collective effort was the participation of Athens, the second largest power and Sparta's rival of long standing. For the time being the Athenians were prepared to defer to Sparta's supreme authority in political and military matters, and the part Athens played in bringing and holding together a united front against the Persians under Spartan leadership cannot be overestimated.[14]

The wartime collaboration can of course be explained easily enough by the sense of urgency which the Persian attack had generated. What is more remarkable is the persistence of political unity beyond the emergency. The long-range effects are well illustrated by the combined Atheno-Spartan efforts, after the expulsion of the Persians, in meting out punishment for *medism* to those Greek states which had defected to the enemy. Athens, then, was still willing to acknowledge Sparta's superiority, conceding to it the role of judge while contenting itself with that of prosecutor. Even as late as approximately 470 unifying sentiments remained strong enough to make the Athenians sacrifice Themistocles, their greatest statesman of the period, on the altar of Panhellenism by exiling him at Sparta's request because of his allegedly pro-Persian inclinations.[15]

Although such continued collaboration may occasion surprise, it can plausibly be argued that there had remained a sufficiently strong residue of anti-Persian feeling to preserve agreement in areas related to the late war. What is more difficult to explain is why, as late as the mid- or late 460's when the emergent rivalry of the two states was becoming increasingly apparent, Athens should still have been willing to comply when Sparta requested aid—not against external enemies but against revolted *perioeci, helots,* and neighbors in the Peloponnese.[16] Treaty obligations alone can hardly furnish an adequate explanation. Spartanophile sentiments of Athenian leaders no doubt did carry considerable weight.[17] But it seems at least possible that the Athenians were also motivated in part by the opportunity to impress their fellow Greeks with their importance for the defense of the homeland should its security be threatened again.

The anti-Persian alliance and the cooperation of the two most powerful states managed to reduce the great diversity among Greek states and create some semblance of political organization. It must also be pointed out, however, that the sense of urgency caused by the barbarian threat was far from universal. A great number of non-Peloponnesian states seemed unable to gauge the full seriousness of the situation and preferred to submit to Persian demands.[18] The oath sworn by the confederates to punish those who had voluntarily submitted to the Persians[19] and the single-mindedness with which punishment was subsequently carried out are a good indication of the continuing political division. The absence of a wider concord no doubt can largely be attributed to Sparta's inadequacy as a leader. But if it is impossible to justify Sparta's failure to offer sufficient encouragement,[20] it must also be said in its defense that the extension of unity to so wide an area was made uncommonly difficult by the sympathy which the Persian cause aroused in oligarchies and most tyrannies. Many of them were ready to pay the fearful price of surrendering their external independence in the expectation that a Persian victory would insure the survival of their political systems.

The picture of Hellenic unity, such as it was, was most clouded by the traditional rivalry between Athens and Sparta, which the emergency had tempered but not eliminated. Early signs of discord can already be detected in the Persian War. Athenian pleas for military aid in the face of Persian preparations for revenge after the defeat at Salamis remained unanswered, possibly because Sparta's interests did not go beyond the defense of the Peloponnese which it expected to accomplish without Athenian help. When Sparta finally granted the requested aid, it did so largely out of fear that its hesitancy might drive the Athenians to join forces with the Persians.[21] An even more drastic expression of Spartan animosity was the insinuation that Athens had deliberately provoked the Persian War to provide an opportunity for its own imperial aggrandizement and thus had selfishly jeopardized the security of all Hellas.[22] The aspersions cast on Athenian sincerity, though unsubstantiated, were not wholly imaginary. Athens, like many other states, did in fact harbor within its walls a pro-Persian party perennially hopeful that Persian aid might make possible the overthrow of democracy;[23] and to make things worse, even the democratic forces had occasionally shown softness toward the Persians in the past. Paradoxical as it may seem, the democratic faction led by Cleisthenes had been responsible for granting the symbols of submission to the Persians in 506–505, in return for aid against a threat emanating from the Peloponnesians and the Central Greeks, while the Panhellenic idea was promoted by Miltiades with the support of the nobility and the peasantry.[24]

However spurious the new unity may have been, the Persian War appreciably reduced the number of independent and disparate power centers. Leaving aside the question of whether subsequent political developments measured up to anticipated goals, the degree of centralization imposed upon the area of Greece by Sparta (with Athenian support) was as novel as it was reassuring, and we can see why a great many voices should have been raised in favor of continuing so beneficial an association even after the invaders had been expelled. However, the eagerness of the Athenians to satisfy such longings was not matched by the sentiments of the Spartans, who by the end of the war had come to distrust profoundly their foremost ally.[25] The rivalry between the two leading cities was not, to be sure, the only reason for the resurgence of particularism. One may indeed wonder whether there had ever existed a sufficient basis for lasting union. Because the notion of a political community was alien, or in any case new, to Greek thinking, the practical value of such unifying factors as blood, language, and religion was limited.[26] The basis of the joint action against the Persians had been chiefly a common dedication to freedom and a fear of

losing it if the union were dissolved.[27] When this common fear
was diminished by the rout of the Persian forces, there was no
longer any basis for continuing the coalition.

BREAKDOWN OF PANHELLENIC CENTRALISM
Decline of Sparta's leadership

If there was no basis in Greek experience and tradition for a
political union of the federative type, one may still wonder why
Sparta, unlike other ancient polities, did nothing to encourage the
incipient trend toward a more comprehensive type of political
organization than the *polis*. The foundation had been propitiously
laid by a great war. Greek particularism notwithstanding, popular
consciousness had accepted the steps taken toward political union
during the war with enough enthusiasm to demur at a return
to the diversified pattern of Greek politics. There is no apparent
reason why Spartan efforts to establish an all-Hellenic state, had
they been made with sufficient vigor, should have miscarried. However, Sparta failed not only to muster the requisite initiative but
also to meet the obligations of leadership under the pressure of war.
We may find it difficult to understand this inertia and wonder
what circumstances prevented Sparta from meeting the challenge
of Athens' rising power, which was the chief stumbling-block to
a united Hellas under Sparta's aegis. It may seem equally strange,
given Sparta's inertia, that Athens should not have replaced it as
the leader of the Hellenic world. Did it not possess wealth and
naval power in excess of what Sparta could match? An examination of the ideal, intellectual, and institutional bases of Greek
politics may shed some light on these questions.

Sparta's leading position was greatly impaired by its evident
lack of enthusiasm in pursuing the Persian War. We are immediately struck by a hesitancy with which it responded both to the
Persian threat and to shifts in the Hellenic balance of power during and after the war, and we may be tempted to conclude that
its leaders failed to grasp the true meaning of events which was
apparent to most Greeks. Actually so harsh a criticism is neither

fair nor accurate. It is impossible not to be impressed by the heroic Spartan resistance at Thermopylae and the inspiration it provided. The deliberate sacrifice not only set a stirring example but also suggested an acute awareness of the gravity of the situation. Nor can one remain oblivious to the leading part played by the Spartans in defeating the Persians at Plataea. However, such displays of concern for the Panhellenic cause were too infrequent to preserve a long-range image of an effective leader. The impression was spreading that Sparta was basically indifferent to the fate of the overseas Greeks[28] and gained momentum as a result of its relapse into seeming inertia after a brief exertion.[29]

Intra-Hellenic problems were attacked with no greater vigor. In consequence, political initiative and leadership in the Persian War could only pass to the Athenians at a time when prudence would have required the exploitation of a unique political opportunity. As a result half the Greek fleet consisted of Athenian ships as early as 480. At Artemisium it was Themistocles, the Athenian general, who made the plans; and Salamis was his show entirely. The Spartans had little choice but to acknowledge and applaud the patriotic role which their inactivity had permitted the Athenians to play and which bestowed upon the rival city the halo of "savior of Hellas."[30]

More than anything else, Sparta's immobility prevented it from playing the part of unifier. Even before the Persian War had come to an end, Sparta had given evidence of its unwillingness or inability to meet the obligations forced upon it by historical circumstances. But if its participation in the defense of Greek lands outside the Peloponnese had been less than wholehearted in the hour of peril, its interest in Panhellenic affairs was further reduced when the acute Persian threat had been removed; this left the continued pursuit of the invader to the Athenians and Ionians.[31] By withdrawing into its isolationist shell Sparta prepared the ground for the rise of a rival who eventually was to threaten its own power. The speeches which Thucydides attributes to the Corinthian emissaries vividly express the exasperation of Sparta's most powerful ally with its leader's complacency in the face of Athens' growing power and ambition.[32] The Athenians, too, used the increasing-ly familiar theme to justify the possession of an empire which Sparta's failure to pursue the barbarians to a decisive defeat had propitiously dropped in their lap.[33] Even in Sparta voices were raised denouncing the apathy which was stymieing the city's foreign policy.[34]

The political consequences of Sparta's lethargy were momentous. On the one hand, this apathy caused many of its allies to defect to the Persians;[35] on the other hand, it greatly strengthened Athens and enabled that state, as a result of its energetic war effort, to advance its political position on two levels. Athens could easily justify suppression of resistance among allies and satellites on the grounds that such resistance was unpatriotic. Furthermore, Athens' decisive part in the defeat of the barbarians, especially its single-handed success at Marathon, justified its claim to equal status with Sparta.[36]

Granting that Sparta's actions and omissions reflect so narrow a range of interests as to make pretensions to a continued monopoly of leadership appear ludicrous, can this be accepted as conclusive evidence that its leaders were lacking political vision? The record does not seem to justify such a judgment. Until the settlement of 446 Sparta's actions clearly imply an acute awareness of the Athenian challenge. Immediately upon termination of the Persian War a determined attempt was made to confine the rival's power by discouraging the restoration of its city walls and to persuade the Athenians to assist in the destruction of the walls of non-Peloponnesian cities.[37] The charge that the Spartans were lacking in political discernment can therefore not be seriously sustained, and we must look elsewhere for explanations of their sterile policy.

The conversion of the once progressive commonwealth into a stagnating oligarchy very probably was brought about by an amalgam of psychological and political factors. No doubt the rigidity of the Spartan constitutional system deserves a fair share of the blame for the paralysis which inhibited the military spirit of its people to the point of self-denial even where impor-tant interests were involved.[38] Designed to perpetuate the rule of the Dorian latecomers over a large indigenous population without political rights, this rigid constitution kept the city on the verge of domestic unrest and absorbed in the military task of maintaining internal peace. There was reason to fear that any extended involvement in remote areas might cause *perioeci* and *helots* to revolt against the small group of Spartan citizens who were keeping them in subjection.[39] This may explain why Sparta passed up the opportunity to encourage defections from its rival's alliance by furnishing promised aid to Thasos when the latter defected from Athens about 465.[40] It is easy to understand that the insecurity of the ruling group deprived Sparta's policy of ingenuity and produced a rigidity which was ill-suited for exercising dominion over the high-spirited and independent Hellenes.[41] What seemed a congenital tendency to avoid risks on closer inspection turns out to be the result of a tenuous social structure and the confining atmosphere of the military state which it had produced.

Internal difficulties, however embarrassing, were not the only reasons for the ineptitude of Sparta's foreign policy. Seemingly incomprehensible blunders frequently were less the result of imprudent choice than of unfavorable international conditions. Sparta's freedom of action was severely restricted by circumstances which were not of its own making and which were not susceptible to immediate correction. The growing independence of states that had recently come into existence or been enlarged handicapped Sparta since progressive democratization frequently resulted.[42] A further handicap was the perennial problem of Argos, which, though a Peloponnesian state, refused to accept Spartan leadership and therefore demanded constant attention.[43] Matters were not helped by the loose structure and the limited purpose of the Peloponnesian League. Aside from the provision that Sparta could not involve its allies in a war without their consent, the usefulness of the league was severely restricted by its lack of naval power.[44] Its effectiveness was further reduced by the allies' hesitancy to assume extra-Peloponnesian commitments.[45] It would have been very unwise for Sparta to assume commitments in remote areas before it had put its own house in order.

If Peloponnesian politics forced Sparta to proceed cautiously in Panhellenic affairs, they obviously did not render it insensitive to problems related to the larger Hellenic balance-of-power system. Efforts to tighten the league were made in the 470's in response to extra-Peloponnesian developments. Further evidence of broader Hellenic interests is not lacking. An anxious concern for Megara, a vital link in the line of communication with the allies in Central Greece; attempts to break the power of Thessaly;[46] and action in the more distant island of Zacynthus in the Ionian Sea[47]— all confirm that Spartan leadership was keeping a watchful eye on events beyond its immediate sphere of influence. Yet Sparta was slow to realize the full seriousness of the Athenian threat. Deceived first by its rival's single-minded dedication to the pursuit of the Persians and later by the temporary stability following the settlement of 446, Sparta did not recognize the bankruptcy of its defensive policy until 433–32, when Athens' power had become a match for the entire Peloponnesian alliance.[48]

The Athenian challenge had two dimensions and was therefore all the more difficult to meet. To contest Athens' maritime supremacy alone was an awe-inspiring prospect. The construction of a first-rate fleet equal to the Athenian fleet in size and quality would not only have been onerous materially, but might also have incurred extensive political liabilities. If the Athenian experience was typical, naval development could be expected to produce democratic tendencies, both at home and elsewhere in the Peloponnese, which Sparta might find difficult, if not impossible, to check.[49] Sparta's stubborn preference for land power must therefore be regarded as more the result of calculation and design than of obtuseness.

Athens' naval power was not, however, the only source of Sparta's troubles. More alarming was the challenge which Athens presented in the realm of politics.[50] The ground had been prepared for political strife in the sixth century when Sparta's hopes to replace the remaining tyrannies everywhere in Hellas with oligarchies fashioned after its own model were only partly realized. Especially disappointing was the decision of the Athenians in favor of a democracy after Sparta had liberated them from tyranny. The Greek states from then on were divided, taking guidance from either the Athenian democracy or the Spartan oligarchy. The partisan strife that revolved about the two competing principles of political organization cleared the way for the dualism that eventually was to tear the Hellenic world asunder.

The very existence of the Athenian democracy, revealing as it did the alluring picture of popular self-government, had a subversive effect upon the peoples of the Peloponnese. By championing the cause of democratic movements, in open revolt against oligarchic rulers everywhere, Athens was able to score political victories even when suffering military setbacks. Sparta did not remain indifferent toward the embarrassment caused by the spreading popularity of the Athenian system. It skillfully maneuvered the aristocrat Cimon into the leading position in Athens in order to take the sting out of the Atheno-Spartan rivalry and end Athenian political agitation in the Peloponnese. The Spartans could perhaps not have foreseen that the maneuver would boomerang. The resourceful Themistocles, exiled from his country upon Sparta's instigation, was now free to tour the Peloponnese, arousing its people against their oligarchic masters.[51] Equally difficult to anticipate was the effect of the democratic development in Athens, which was soon to render Cimon's position untenable.[52] The failure of this policy was a serious setback for Sparta. Its rigid institutions and its leadership of a confederacy of oligarchies prevented it from meeting the democratic challenge with more forceful means than by extolling the superior virtues of its own political system and by a commitment to defend it.[53] This approach could not but miss its mark once it had become clear that Sparta's legendary constitutional order, like most others, had been unable to withstand the general moral and social decay of the period.

Although Sparta was thus caught up in many more or less uncontrollable predicaments, there can be little question that its inaction in Panhellenic matters must bear the chief responsibility for making the emergence of a power dualism possible. This was serious enough in itself. But indecision in foreign affairs had also generated much wishful thinking among its leaders. Unable or unwilling to face reality in estimating the relative power of naval and land arms, they had failed to provide adequately for the event of a war with Athens, as the dismal state of Sparta's preparedness at the outbreak of the war amply illustrates.[54] What better evidence of the Spartan capacity for self-delusion could be cited than the fatuous hope of Archidamus, the Spartan king who led the invading forces, that even after war had been declared and the invasion of Attica begun, a military clash might still be avoided? [55] No doubt his contention that what appeared to be procrastination in actual fact was the wisest moderation (*malista sophrosyne*)[56] merits consideration. But under the circumstances one must wonder whether Sparta's hesitancy still bore any relationship to the problems of the day. It is difficult to escape the impression that at a time when all Hellas was drifting toward the abyss, Sparta's foreign policy remained aimless.[57]

The Athenian challenge

It may seem odd that of all the Greek states Athens should have been the one to challenge Sparta's leadership. The city's beginnings had not been auspicious. Not only had Attica's rise been delayed by political strife,[58] but the area had been in economic distress almost from the beginning.[59] Although these handicaps were frequently a source of embarrassment to Athenian foreign policy during the period from 476 to 446,[60] they were amply offset by other factors favoring a rapid development. Perhaps the city's most obvious natural advantage was its geographic location in the crossroads of Dorian and Ionian cultural currents.[61] But if one looks a little deeper, even the seeming disadvantages of its early history turn out to be valuable assets. Perhaps the period of hardships supplied the stimulus for Athens to take advantage of the opportunity for greatness which the Persian War provided.

Athens had long been in the front ranks of Greek states. In the Persian War it attained a leading position. At that time its main strength was the quality of its statesmanship, which was quick to grasp the seriousness of the Persian threat and to see the need for concerted action. The bravery and resourcefulness displayed at Marathon and Salamis fully justified its aspiration to play a leading part in Hellenic affairs. Most of Hellas probably felt, as did Herodotus, that the Athenian contribution had been the saving grace.[62] Even Sparta would have been hard put to deny, without incurring the opprobrium of petty jealousy, the eminent part played by the Athenians in the joint action of 481–80 and in the direction of the campaign of 480–79.

The Athenians were not moved by altruism or dreams of heroic grandeur alone, but also by considerations of a pragmatic nature. The threat which Persian despotism represented to their newly acquired democracy must have been a strong motivation to resist the invader.[63] But whatever selfish considerations may have moved them, it was easy enough to disguise such motives with the Panhellenic cloak that was readily available to the protagonist of the common cause. Athenian ambitions to rise to the heights traditionally occupied by Sparta were aided by the latter's failure to seize this opportunity for forging Hellenic unity. It is hard to imagine that Athens could have become the champion of the Greek cause had not Sparta relinquished its defense before the job was finished. But with Sparta's premature *de facto* resignation from leadership, the foundation was laid for the subsequent hegemonial claims of the Athenians.[64]

The ultimate reason for Athens' rise to a leading position was probably more political than military. It was less military valor than the decision to assume the guardianship of Hellenic freedom which Sparta had abandoned that accounted for Athens' success. But aside from calculation and determination Athens was also favored by a fundamental change in Greek military technology which had occurred during the war. For the first time, naval power had come into its own. Before the war chances that Sparta's military supremacy could be challenged on the sea would have been slight. But now the sea had clearly emerged as a new and perhaps more important dimension of military power.[65] Even if Sparta had possessed greater initiative than it did, it might not have been able to meet this fortuitous development which so greatly favored its rival.

The changed military technology and Athens' new exalted position were to have a profound impact on its domestic as well as foreign policy. To be sure, a new direction had been given to the structure of Athenian society as early as the end of the sixth century when Themistocles had succeeded in persuading his countrymen to build a navy. But the democratic tendencies which gained ground from then on were given further impetus by the burst of activity in naval construction and commerce which followed the Persian War. It was not surprising that the new activities raised the lower strata of society to positions of increased economic and military importance. Less immediately apparent, but perhaps even more consequential, was the effect of the new direction in the realm of thought. The improved economic and political status of the lower classes was to bring forth much optimism concerning man's ability to master his fate.[66] Such self-reliance easily generated the belief that mere activity, even if aimless, could sustain continuous progress. In this respect the new mode of thought was not unlike modern progressivist ideologies. To be sure, progress was hardly considered a moral or political dogma, based on the presumed knowledge of ultimate truth, as is modern progressivism. What was similar was the tendency to accept the new as a good in itself measured by no other standard than its place in the progression of time.

In thus releasing Athenian society from traditional restraints, the new democracy was generating much nervous and noncreative activity which could not fail to have unsettling political implications. But the more immediate benefits of progressivism overshadowed its long-range disadvantages. The political and strategic advances following in its wake were considerable and elicited words of praise even from as severe a critic as Aristotle.[67] In raising the ambitions of the city to new heights it was fostering a strong sense of civic obligation; and the democratic faith in progress was bringing to the surface a mass of talent which was to contribute far more imagination and enterprise than could be mustered by the rigid oligarchies.[68]

In foreign relations, too, the new spirit made its imprint. Above all it was responsible for awakening the Athenians to the political opportunity of assuming the protectorate of the insular Ionian and Aeolian allies and thus making themselves into a veritable symbol of anti-Persian resistance. The freedom from Persian rule which the overseas Greeks had just won had little tangible value unless the victory were secured through a permanent and enlarged Hellenic federation which included them. Sparta was not oblivious to the need for extending the security sphere beyond the Greek mainland; but being a land power, it was ill-equipped to do so effectively.[69] The best it could do was offer a plan for a Greek-Persian disengagement through a population transfer of overseas Greeks to the European mainland. Such a plan could hardly have had a great appeal to the exposed insulars while Athens was standing ready to guarantee protection for their homes overseas.[70]

The establishment of the protectorate proved a boon to Athens, and appears to have been the decisive step toward dual hegemony. Under the pressure of the emergency, it probably occurred to few that the new protector was likely to nurture ambitions of its own. Yet a realistic interpretation of political events should have anticipated that the newly gained power and prestige would whet the appetite of the Athenians for territorial acquisitions and that in the course of time the protectorates were likely means to satisfy such longings.[71] As later developments were to show, the strengthening of the bond with the insular kinsmen, which would surely have been severed had they been transplanted to Europe under Spartan auspices,[72] turned out to be the chief support on which Athenian power rested.

The Athenian protectorate over the Ionian Greeks was soon institutionalized through the Delian League, formed about 478–77 as a roof organization for the maritime Greeks. There is no reason to doubt Thucydides' assertion that the organization had its origin in the voluntary act of the allies.[73] A vast amount of good will had been generated by Athens' declared willingness to hold its unmatched naval power ready for their continued protection.[74] The Athenians were unwavering in their hostility toward the Persians and able to hold the enemy at bay, as their performance at Marathon had demonstrated. Athenian protection was doubly welcomed because it would relieve the overseas Greeks from the violence they had been made to suffer at the hands of the Spartan regent Pausanias.[75] But to say that the formation of the league was voluntary is not to imply that the part played by the Athenians was purely negative. The formation of the league with Athens as its leader was in fact the natural sequel to Athens' construction of a superior navy and the assumption of naval leadership during the Persian War, followed by Athens' promise to defend the integrity of the maritime Greeks. In guiding Athenian policy along these lines, Themistocles no doubt had envisaged the eventual establishment of formal ties with the allies, which would reinforce Athens' *de facto* with *de jure* dominance; and many of his fellow citizens shared his vision.

It would be futile here to resume the argument whether the Delian League was an organization within the larger framework of the Hellenic League, as has often been contended, or whether it was an independent alliance replacing the Hellenic League in the pursuit of the war against the Persians.[76] Such an inquiry would accomplish no more than a clarification of formal rights and obligations. Of more concern here are substantive political relations, which often are too subtle and fluctuating to be stated precisely. The most that can be said is that the ostensible purpose of the new league to retaliate for Persian ravages[77] was entirely compatible with the goals of the Panhellenic system and that its formation did not in itself constitute an act of secession. But if the Delian League was professedly anti-Persian in its initial conception, Themistocles and Cimon, the two leaders who had the greatest influence upon the shaping of Athenian foreign policy during the postwar period, were at variance concerning its long-term aims. Committed to the Panhellenic cause, Cimon persevered in a policy of friendship toward Sparta. By contrast, Themistocles was anticipating the likelihood of a showdown between the two leading Greek powers. His policy was therefore oriented toward promoting the particularistic interests of Athens, even though this would necessarily weaken the Panhellenic cause.[78]

While Themistocles was in exile, Cimon's point won out and formed the temporary basis of Athenian policy. However, in the long run Themistocles' aims could not fail to come to fruition. The appearance of unity among the members of the Hellenic League, which seems to have been preserved until the formal break about 462,[79] cannot conceal the competitive spirit that possessed the Athenians vis-à-vis their Spartan allies. The admission of the Ionian Greeks (via the Delian League) to active membership in the concert of Hellenic powers, which Themistocles had ardently advocated,[80] evidently was designed to tip the balance of power in Athens' favor.

The division of power between a land and a maritime hegemony and the divided allegiance of the allies could not but undermine the cohesion of the Panhellenic organization and bring to the surface the open rivalry between the naval league of the Athenians and the Peloponnesian Confederacy headed by Sparta. However, the responsibility for the breakup of Hellenic unity cannot be wholly ascribed to Themistocles and his followers. To a large extent it was the result of the political conditions which the Persian War had produced. Ironically enough, Cimon and his Spartanophile faction contributed more than a modest share to the growing Atheno-Spartan rivalry by actively promoting Athenian expansionism.[81] In response to the progressive bipolarization of power along the land-sea divide, Sparta endeavored to counterbalance Athenian power by extending its influence on land to Central Greece and Thessaly.[82]

Its declared anti-Persian orientation did not prevent the Delian League from eventually becoming an instrument for realizing Athens' ambitions in Hellas proper. The loose and voluntary organization founded on the principle of equality was soon converted into a closely knit unit doing Athens' bidding. The allies may have been surprised to find that in some respects the earlier

appearance of voluntarism had been deceiving. If they had believed they were free to secede, they were overlooking the techni-
cality that the alliance was not contingent upon the continuance
of the Persian threat, but had been concluded in perpetuity. They
were soon to learn from the punitive actions with which Athens
met the attempted defections of Naxos and Thasos in 470 and
465 respectively that the leading power was not prepared to tolerate assertions of independence. It also became clear before long
that the league was capable of virtually unlimited growth and
ready to receive any insular or overseas state which Athens chose
to designate for membership. Where persuasion did not succeed,
the armed force of the league was usually sufficient to break the
resistance of the unwilling.

It was probably no mere coincidence that the tightening of
Athens' hold over the allies followed the transition from a purely
anti-Persian policy to one that was anti-Spartan as well. Efforts
to secure and extend the Athenian hegemony gained in intensity
after the conclusion of the so-called Peace of Callias with the
Persians in 449.[83] The reason is not difficult to see. In most cases
the fear of an alien despotism had been strong enough to make
the allies toe the line; but as the league was increasingly diverted
to anti-Spartan ends, no such fear could be relied upon to maintain discipline and solidarity. The onerous obligations of membership, consisting of contributions to the common defense in the
form of ships or money, had been a source of much discontent
while the danger of Persian conquest was still acute. But with the
rout of the Persian forces at the Eurymedon River about 467, it
was felt increasingly that all reason for continued deference to
the protector's dictation had vanished.[84] However, if such was
the view held by the allies, it was not shared by the Athenians, who
had no intention to abandon an organization needed to further
their political ambitions. Determined to hold the league together
irrespective of the recession of the Persian threat, they were prepared to proceed with the utmost ruthlessness if necessary.

The regime which Athens established throughout the league
clearly reflects the evaporation of the allies' autonomy. From the

outset a centralizing trend was apparent in the making of the organization's policy. It was not long before the Athenian *ecclesia* virtually displaced the allied *synhedrion* by assuming legislative authority over defected states and allies of dubious loyalty.[85] The *ecclesia* also exercised discretion in setting the tributes payable by the allies and in allocating confederate funds.[86] In 454 Athenian control over the league's funds was further tightened when the confederate treasury was transferred from the island of Delos to Athens. The transfer ostensibly was undertaken to provide greater security since the islands were left exposed to Persian or Phoenician attacks after the débâcle which the Athenian forces had suffered earlier that year in Egypt. No doubt there was much plausibility in the strategic argument invoked to justify the transfer. However, the very fact that Athens became the depository of the league's vast funds necessarily gave the Athenians more perfect control than they had before, not only over the treasury but also over the allies.

The Athenians did not rely on financial means alone to secure their control over the league; where circumstances seemed to demand it, they readily encroached upon their allies' autonomy in the military and political spheres. To facilitate what we might call "federal execution," doubtful allies were compelled to tear down city walls and to admit Attic garrisons temporarily. Athenian supremacy was formally secured through the transfer of criminal jurisdiction for almost the entire league area to Athenian courts and through the introduction of Attic coinage and standards of weights and measures. It also seems that beginning in the late 450's and early 440's the Athenians attempted to cement their alliances through more or less forcible adaptation of allied political systems to Athens' own democratic constitution. Although modern knowledge of the history of the period is far from complete, inscriptional evidence exists in the case of Erythrae, Colophon, and Chalcis.[87] Evidently it was hoped that the control of governments by popular parties would insure pro-Athenian sympathies, as there was reason to fear that oligarchic governments would be impervious to Athenian influence.[88] Insistence on democratic constitutions in allied cities eventually was to become a preferred Athenian policy, and it appears that by 446–45 treaties with new allies normally included commitments concerning their internal political organization. By appealing to the people and creating the expectation that a close link with the democratic metropolis would protect them against oligarchic takeovers, Athens evidently hoped to make sure that its allies would be its willing tools.

After 450 the practice of settling Attic citizens (*cleruchoi*) in conquered or subjected areas was gaining favor as a means of securing the empire. One reason for such settlements may of course have been the desire to relieve the misery of the Athenian poor by giving them a gratuity at the expense of some allied city. But there is little doubt that the chief function of the *cleruchoi* was to guard the league against subversion.[89] One important difference between the *cleruchies* and the older Greek practice of establishing colonies (*apoikiai*) overseas underscores the former's political purpose. The rationale behind the *apoikia* was generally economic, and since its sole purpose was to relieve the population pressure in the metropolis, there was no reason to deny it political independence. The status of the *cleruchies* was different inasmuch as the *cleruchs* retained their Attic citizenship and their land remained under Athenian jurisdiction.

This sketchy account of the relations between the Athenians and their allies makes no pretense of completeness. The object is to point out the changes in purpose and power structure of the Delian League which occurred between its founding and the outbreak of the Peloponnesian War. The development shows that the long-range goal of resisting Persian encroachments was gradually displaced by efforts to augment Athenian strength in relation to Sparta. From the short-term point of view the league had become an instrument for disciplining rebellious members, reducing most allies, in effect, to the status of Athenian satellites. There was little the allies could do to resist Athenian infringements upon their autonomy. In entering the alliance they had obligated themselves to contribute to the common defense. As time went on and the resumption of a Persian attack appeared an increasingly remote possibility, a growing number of allies substituted monetary for military contributions, either because Athens so desired or because they were anxious to turn their energies to peacetime activities. They may have been unaware that in doing so they were helping the Athenians establish a monopoly of effective striking power while stripping themselves of the capability to resist. By 454 only the islands of Chios, Lesbos, and Samos had remained contributors of ships and crews; the remaining allies had been converted, usually with their own consent, into tribute-paying members. The growing resources of the league, almost entirely at the disposal of Athens, encouraged harsh enforcement action against delinquent members and produced the general consensus in Hellas that the Delian League had become an empire in fact.

COULD BIPOLARISM HAVE BEEN PREVENTED?

By 446 the Athenian empire was complete. Sparta's leadership had been finally and openly displaced by a dual hegemony. The events leading to the bipolarization of power are easy enough to discern; however, it is more difficult to ascertain whether it could have been avoided had the leading powers acted with more circumspection than they did. The history of the interwar years shows neither that the bipolar constellation emerged by accident nor that it was the necessary result of the political division between the masses and the oligarchs, which was assuming a growing importance in most Greek cities. Events point more definitely to causes inherent in military circumstances and international combinations. It is unlikely that bipolarization would have occurred had not the Persian War furnished the necessary background of political unity and precipitated a military development that was to encourage a division of functions between Sparta and Athens.

This wider context must be considered in assessing responsibility for the emergence of the bipolar alignment. The new trend cannot be attributed to Sparta's complacency so clearly and directly as surface appearances suggest. It is true enough that during the years following the rout of the Persians Sparta proved unequal to the task of reversing the political and military trend that was favoring Athens. But it must be recalled that Sparta's freedom of action was severely restricted by circumstances which could not be made to yield with sufficient speed to meet new and unforeseen conditions.

One way of avoiding bipolarization would have been to keep the wartime alliance intact. However, it is the common fate of such alliances to disintegrate once the enemy has been defeated. The Panhellenic League was no exception, and it is difficult to see what Sparta could have done to keep Athens in a subordinate position permanently. The Spartans certainly cannot be accused of being oblivious to the rapidly growing ambitions of the Athenians, and they did make numerous attempts to mend their fences. The failure of such efforts and Sparta's eventual resignation can ultimately be ascribed to the nature of its political order and the character of the Peloponnesian League. Both had their roots in Sparta's history and were, in a sense, of its own making. But whatever the origin of such adverse conditions, they were not something that could be changed on short notice. It was only natural that the maritime allies should have sought protection behind the shield of Athens' unique naval power. Without a comparable naval force Sparta was in no position to reverse the alignment through diplomatic or belligerent means. There were no grounds for challenging the formation of a league based on its members' freely given consent, and in the absence of concrete provocations belligerent action would not have been promising. What is more, an unprovoked war would have shattered Sparta's political image as the professed liberator of Hellas from fear and oppression, which was its chief political asset.

Sparta's inaction gave the Athenians the opportunity to fashion Greek international politics in their own style. Events might, of course, have taken a different turn had Athens failed to rise to the Persian challenge and neglected the development of its naval power. In that event either Sparta's leadership would have endured or Hellas would have remained a politically dispersed geographic area. Under conditions of Hellenic disunity, a Persian victory and the

resulting loss of Hellenic identity would have been the likely outcome. As it was, Athens, which had just become conscious of its
new power, unfolded an extraordinary vitality that would not
let it remain inactive in the face of the opportunities presented
by the Persian attack. The general effect of its successes in the
war was to generate expansionist tendencies having less specific
purpose than the campaign against the Persians.

Athens' expansionism was aimed chiefly at the nearby Greeks and
was bound to result in conflict with Sparta. To be sure, the resolve
to expand in the direction of its Greek neighbors was not altogether
capricious. It was the inevitable consequence of the Athenian
protectorate over the Ionians. If that obligation was to be dis-
charged effectively, the protector had to be prepared to undertake
military expeditions into remote areas, and this necessitated the
establishment of security at home by insuring the cooperation of
as many Greek cities as possible. But the Athenians were soon to
discover that they had overextended themselves. When their
quest for hegemony led to a formal break with Sparta, they found
themselves involved in a simultaneous two-front war against
Persia and Sparta which clearly exceeded their capabilities. They
therefore had little choice but to stabilize the existing situation by
reaching agreements with both their opponents: the so-called Peace
of Callias with the Persians in about 449 and the general settlement
with Sparta in 446–45. The Athenian drive for power had thus
temporarily come to a standstill.

There was nevertheless no lack of opportunity for Athens to
attain supremacy. Probably the most promising moment for reducing Sparta to a second-rate power came in 464 when the dual
impact of an earthquake and a *helots'* revolt was seriously impair-
ing its striking power.[90] Athens could then have tried at small
cost to exploit Sparta's temporary weakness. Domestic politics
prevented this. This was the time when Themistocles, the spokes-
man for the anti-Spartan faction, was in exile and the Spartanophile
Cimon was the leading political figure in Athens. The crucial event
of the period then appears to be the success of the pro-Spartan
party in exiling Themistocles, whose banishment was tantamount

to the abandonment of Athenian aspirations to the mastery of Hellas during most of the decade. In historical perspective Themistocles' vision seems the more realistic; Cimon's dream of perpetual friendship with Sparta under a dualism of power appears to have made little sense in view of Athens' enormous vitality and physical growth. Although Cimon eventually was punished with ostracism for his limited vision, the propitious moment for seizing supremacy could not be recaptured after Athens was led back on the course which Themistocles had charted for it.

The fifty years between the Persian War and the Peloponnesian War thus appear as a history of missed opportunities which, if seized with determination, might have led to the clear supremacy of one of the two rivals. Although political leaders cannot be absolved entirely of responsibility for failing to squelch emergent bipolar tendencies, it is evident that there existed a set of political and military circumstances which strongly favored the rise of such a system. It did not take much in the way of personal omissions or miscalculations to clear the road for that development. The results of the deep and unbridgeable cleavages were two societies with different political preferences and irreconcilable interests, whose bitter strife eventually was to reduce Hellas to the point of physical and political exhaustion from which it was never fully to recover.

chapter 3

THE CONTEST

THE COLD WAR

The Persian War had brought about a redistribution of power in Greece. Within fifteen years after the rout of the enemy, the dual leadership hardened to form a distinct and widely acknowledged pattern. The novel relationships between the two leading powers as well as between them and the lesser states were to create problems of a new type. Much uncertainty and confusion was bound to arise from the new kind of international relations which rendered obsolete the familiar categories of war and peace. Except for the few years from 457 until the signing of the five years' truce in 453 or 451 (the date is uncertain), no formal state of war seems to have existed between Athens and Sparta; and even the military clashes of those years appear more as a series of individual actions to improve strategic positions than as part of a comprehensive plan to crush the opponent's resistance. At the same time, the turbulent fifty-year period between the wars was definitely not one of peace in the usual sense.

The state of affairs, which was neither *de jure* war nor *de facto* peace, perhaps comes closest to what we would call "cold war" today. To this it may be objected that deep-seated suspicions and even bitter animosities were entirely normal in the relations between Greek states and that there was nothing extraordinary about an uneasy calm constantly on the verge of erupting into open conflict. Hence the interwar period formed no exception to what was customarily known as a state of peace, furnishing no basis for special categorization. The argument is not without merit. However, the presence of tension and competition was not peculiar to the "normal" relations between Greek states. Peace in general is often far from being the tranquil state of affairs that it may appear, and the dividing line between peace and war is almost always tenuous. But if the difference is essentially one of degree, the same relativity applies to the distinction between peace and cold war. The question of whether the latter category is here applicable, then, depends on the presence of sufficiently unique characteristics to make such a distinction meaningful.

The first thing to be noted in surveying the period is the appearance of a new temper, gaining in intensity as time progressed, marked by an excessively competitive spirit. Outwardly the new temper manifested itself in the unprecedented enormity of military preparations made by Athens and Sparta as the redistribution of power was crystalizing. The reason for stepping up armaments evidently lay in an entirely realistic assessment of the new political situation, created by the emergence of two equal superpowers, in which an approximate military equilibrium seemed the only insurance of some measure of stability. It was therefore not so much a craving for prestige as a desperate concern for political survival that was responsible for the armaments race. The possibility that the opponent might gain a limitless and enduring supremacy no doubt was frightening to both sides. In the tug of war that ensued, outside help could not be counted on. Although the lesser states were to play an important part in the contest, their potential material contributions were not such as to justify a relaxation of efforts. Neither was there much hope that any third power or group of powers might gain sufficient strength to act as an effective balancer.

The contestants thus were forced to depend largely on their own devices. To relax vigilance and military preparations in a situation so fraught with uncertainty might have been disastrous.

Even if Sparta on occasion seemed to slacken its efforts, it did so, as has been seen, largely because its hands were tied. As the conflict sharpened, both felt the urgent need to push ahead with increasing truculence in order to exploit every advantage vis-à-vis the opponent as well as third states. Considering the magnitude of the anxieties and animosities generated, it is hardly surprising that tensions were heightened almost to the limit of endurance. It is also easy to understand that in the face of the struggle between the giants, particularistic interests and the contentiousness of lesser states were wholly subordinated to the bipolar cold war context.

Under these circumstances there seemed to be small chance that either military efforts or political tensions might be relaxed. The stakes involved were high, and extreme military preparedness alone could furnish a reasonable sense of security. The fears that were responsible for the military competition were also reflected in the political sphere. A tendency on both sides to magnify even the most minute changes, because of the real or imaginary effect they might have upon the political balance, precluded any significant compromise. Open war was nevertheless avoided for an extended period, probably because the approximate military equilibrium precluded any confident anticipation of its outcome. Under such sustained tensions, military clashes could not always be avoided, of course. But as long as neither of the adversaries was ready for the final showdown, the chief struggle remained in the realm of politics. The subordinate role of war in the military sense did not, to be sure, justify undue optimism. The uncompromising attitude of the contestants was enough to keep international relations in a sustained state of crisis, subject to being escalated into full-fledged war at almost any time. The warlike atmosphere and heightened sensibilities hardly presented a picture of conventional peace.

Consolidation of the Athenian position

Three phases of the cold war can easily be distinguished. The years from 478 to 462 were marked by unilateral Athenian activity and a relative lethargy on the part of the Spartans. Between

462 and 446 we can perceive a general awakening of the Hellenic world to the new alignment of powers and an increasing assumption of initiative by Sparta. This spurt of activity was followed by a studious avoidance of provocations by both antagonists from 446 to 431.

During the first phase, immediately following the Persian War, the initiative in Greek international relations belonged to Athens. Themistocles, then the leading statesman, carefully avoided any move that might seriously provoke Sparta, though he did endeavor to fortify his city's position by strengthening its naval power and extending its control in Asia Minor through conquests and alliances. While engaged in consolidating its power along the fringes, Athens refrained from causing unnecessary disturbances in the homeland and adjacent waters. The only actions close to home during the first postwar decade were the forcible integration of Carystus (on the southern tip of neighboring Euboea) into the Delian League for better protection against enemy attacks[1] and the subjection of Naxos, which had defected from the league.[2] In this way Athens preserved a tenuous calm, which could hardly be expected to last in view of Sparta's awkward situation in the new scheme of things. The causes of the eventual eruption are complex and require elaboration in some detail.

Under the bipolar configuration that had emerged from the unity prevailing under its aegis during the Persian War, Sparta quite naturally wanted to defend the status quo, which so greatly favored it. Although its position no longer was as unassailable as it had been before the war, Sparta could still lay good moral and legal claims to political supremacy. It therefore seemed important to thwart further Athenian inroads in order to salvage the essential foundations of the old order. This was not, however, an easy thing to do. Encouraged by their successes in the Persian War, the Athenians persisted in efforts to upset the customary distribution of power. The risks for Athens were small; except for a premature involvement in a war, it had little to lose. At worst, things would remain as they were, and almost any change would be to Athens' advantage. The alternatives available to the

Spartans were not so clearcut. Any serious attempt to checkmate Athenian advances implied grave risks. Hazardous expeditions against the powerful adversary might not only have jeopardized Sparta's leading position but also have invited general disaster. With the naval hegemony in Athenian hands and in view of domestic difficulties, it seemed best to stick to a defensive policy, even if it is arguable whether this was the only or the wisest choice. Sparta's major allies, the Corinthians, for example, apparently did not consider it a wise choice, as their persistent charges of deliberate procrastination, reported by Thucydides, indicate.[3]

Sparta's predicament was serious. Unless it was willing to seize the initiative, it could scarcely expect to assert its leadership indefinitely. A purely defensive policy of simply responding to Athenian challenges provided no formula for meeting the situation which Athenian aggressiveness had created. But in taking the risks which positive action implied, Sparta would have found its freedom of action restricted by its commitment to the status quo, since specific incidents that would justify military action against the restless Athenians could not always be isolated. We have already spoken of the embarrassment created by the formation of the Delian League, confronting Sparta with an accomplished fact which, however disagreeable, it could do little to reverse without committing aggression. To be guilty of seemingly unprovoked belligerency would have put the presumed guardian of Hellenic freedom and of the existing order in a wholly untenable moral and political position. Therefore, as long as Athens managed to avoid the charge of outright aggression, Sparta was doomed to inactivity.

Under the circumstances, Athens found it advantageous to refrain from direct provocations. Its aggressiveness continued ostensibly to be directed toward the common Persian enemy. In actuality, the weaker Greek states were the objects of Athens' ambition. The subjection of fellow Greeks could be justified in the eyes of the world through reference to the natural order of things, which favors the strong. The Athenians tried to make such cold rationalization palatable by contending that their mastery was benevolently tempered by enlighted rule.[4] To such specious argu-

ments Sparta could offer little more than the promise to preserve formal freedom. However, these promises were bound to lose
persuasiveness in view of Sparta's inability to combat the more
subtle means the Athenians employed in reducing Greek states to
the status of *de facto* dependencies.

Sparta's predicament stands out clearly in the Naxos incident.
Here was a unique opportunity to intervene in the face of the
savage subjugation of an autonomous Greek state by the Athenians.
Unfortunately for Sparta as well as for Naxos, even if the legality
of the Athenian action may be a moot point,[5] the law was not all
on the victim's side. The fact that the Naxians had broken their
treaty obligations created an awkward situation. Intercession in
their behalf would have left the Spartans open to the charge of
promoting lawlessness and thereby undermining the status quo.
Aid to Naxos could therefore have been justified only in terms
of a full-blown policy of containment, such as was not developed
until later.

During the years from 462 to 446, after the crucial defeat of
the Persians by the Athenians, Sparta's political outlook seems to
have changed. The unlikelihood of further Persian attacks in the
near future had reduced the need for continued Atheno-Spartan
solidarity. The Spartans' new estimate of the situation was confirmed by the mounting pressure that was emanating from Athenian quarters. Although it is by no means certain that encroachments upon Sparta's land hegemony had been part of the Athenian
design initially, the possession of a navy of such gigantic proportions was to increase the scope of their ambitions to a point where
it became a generally disturbing factor in the Hellenic world.[6]

The transition of Athenian policy from a purely anti-Persian
to an anti-Spartan orientation was gradual and sporadic, as the
Spartanophiles were still commanding considerable respect at home.
However, the Athenians did not remain content with consolidating
their maritime position, but eventually tried to edge in on the sphere
the Spartans had staked out for themselves.[7] The ostracism of
Athens' leader Cimon in 461 openly marks the break with the
former ally.[8] The year 458–57 found Athens at the head of

a land confederacy—supported by the Peloponnesian city of Argos—including Megarians, Boeotians, Phocaeans, and Opuntian Locrians.[9] These new alliances sooner or later were to involve Athens in clashes with the Peloponnesian Confederacy. In the face of Athenian inroads into its domain Sparta could no longer remain passive, and by 457 it was ready to enter the struggle.[10] But despite its readiness to meet the adversary on the field of battle, Sparta still appears to have shown little genuine alarm. The victory at Tanagra was not exploited, and the gains made were soon wiped out by the Athenian victory at Oenophyta.[11] The Corinthians were alarmed and for good reason. Athens had acquired footholds along the Peloponnesian coast and elsewhere which threatened to isolate the Peloponnese from the outside world. Also, Corinth's colonial empire was struck a serious blow when the western islands of Zacynthus and Cephallenia joined Athens about 456.[12] Still, the Spartans do not appear to have had a comprehensive plan for meeting the Athenian challenge head-on. They preferred to indulge the vague hope that opportunities to station sizable military contingents in the vicinity of Attica would set off a revolution in Athens which would relieve them of the need for a military attack. If such hopes had any basis, they were ultimately dashed by the inefficacy of the Athenian oligarchs.[13]

Sparta's lethargy, based on miscalculation, false illusions, and domestic pressures, especially after the exhausting siege of Ithome, largely accounts for the success of Athens' foreign policy. The Spartans had good reason to refrain from militarily engaging the rival city at the height of its strength, but it is not so easy to understand Sparta's continued reserve after the Athenian expeditionary forces had suffered serious reverses in Egypt in 454–53. The defeat had undermined the allies' confidence in Athens' ability to provide effective protection and thereby seriously impaired its hegemonial control. It may seem strange that under these auspicious circumstances Sparta failed to take advantage of its rival's temporary paralysis. Yet closer inspection reveals reasons for its failure to do so which cannot be easily dismissed. The disaster had raised anew the spectre of a Persian attack, and Spartan statesmen must have had serious doubts concerning their city's ability to ward off the enemy without the aid of the Athenian navy.[14] Although it may have been entirely possible to eliminate the annoying rival, an armistice must have appeared preferable. What is more perplexing at first sight is the continued absence of any serious Spartan attempt to reduce the opponent when the Persian threat had receded and Athens was further weakened during the following years. This persistent inertia in fact made it possible for the Athenians to consolidate their power.

In retrospect Sparta's course actually seems sensible enough, even if it exasperated its allies. A showdown with Athens would have necessitated the destruction of its navy, and Sparta's land forces could not have accomplished that.[15] It therefore seemed more politic to terminate hostilities. In 446 a treaty of settlement was concluded which essentially restored the status quo of the period before 462. Under its terms Athens was to surrender all its strongholds in the Peloponnese and some in Central Greece as well as Megara. Moreover, the contracting parties were not to attack each other or to give support to or admit to their respective alliance systems any of their treaty partner's defected allies, though they remained free to enter into alliances with uncommitted states. Any dispute arising between them was to be settled through arbitration.

If the settlement appears to have met Sparta's needs, can it be said that it served Athens' interests equally well? The question will have to be answered affirmatively. The agreement actually saved Athens from a very serious situation.[16] The simultaneous struggle against Persians and Spartans between 477 and 449 had accomplished little, and Athenian statesmen had come to realize that the two-pronged war could not be continued indefinitely without serious risks. A clarification of policy, by assigning priorities to the two distinct goals, was therefore imperative. Opinions may have been divided as to the desirable order of priority. But Pericles above all Athenian statesmen apparently felt that the immediate contest would have to be with Sparta for hegemony in Hellas.[17] The eventual decision in favor of an exclusively anti-Spartan orientation was followed by the Peace of Callias with the Persian king

in 449. Although there may be some doubt that the peace signified a major triumph, it served Athens' political interests admirably by permitting it to prepare for the intra-Hellenic competition. At the same time it was deemed advisable, even after the
immobilization of the Persian front, not to continue the indecisive
contest with Sparta which had left both the Athenian fleet and the
Peloponnesian army intact.[18] In offering Sparta the settlement
Athens no doubt hoped to be able to pursue its policy more effectively through political rather than military means.[19] Although
the treaty was far from favorable, it did give Athens what it
needed most: time to strengthen and develop its naval power.

Glancing back over this period of military clashes, the one salient
point that stands out is the inordinate instability in the alignment
of powers. The frequent fluctuations seem to have been induced
by the contestants' eagerness to welcome the opponent's disaffected
allies and friends into their respective alliance systems. That ready
hospitality was the natural result of the rivalry between the big
powers, which was gaining in intensity as the bipolar pattern
was hardening and which would not let either be content with
the protection of its respective domain. Because of the mounting
political competition Athens would not tolerate defections from
the Delian League. But it also felt a compulsive urge to extend
the sphere of its control whenever and wherever this was possible.
Sparta's objectives too transcended the mere protection of the
Peloponnesian Confederacy. In order to forestall a major upset of
the increasingly precarious power equilibrium, it was no less anxious
than Athens to win new friends and allies. The expansionist policies
of the leading states alone were enough to cause considerable political vacillation. But a further element of unrest was introduced
by the self-assertion and occasional belligerency of the lesser states,
in response to the encouragement which the big power competition
was providing.

Stabilization of the bipolar balance

With the settlement of 446 the bipolar pattern was recognized
in form as well as in fact. Athens now abandoned its imperialistic

designs on land, limiting itself to the pursuit of a naval empire, for which it had obtained Sparta's formal recognition.[20] However, the two spheres of domination on land and on the sea, formally recognized by the treaty, were not clearly staked out or delineated, and no Iron Curtain was rung down. Although both treaty partners undertook not to admit their opponent's defected allies to their respective alliance systems, the treaty provided for freedom to solicit uncommitted cities. At first sight, the settlement would appear to fit rather admirably the political needs of the moment; Sparta's evident expectation that the bipolar balance might be stabilized by recognizing and simultaneously containing Athens' maritime empire did not seem unreasonable. Since the dualism of power was now complete, prospects for an enduring peace appeared rather promising if only Athens would respect the newly created status quo.[21] However, such hopes proved vain. Fears and points of friction had not been removed, and the tug of war between the Big Two continued for several more or less obvious reasons. The restless and self-perpetuating activity which the naval development had generated permitted no rest to the Athenians themselves or to others. Although the initial effect of this activity was merely to stimulate the progressive democratization of Athens' internal power structure, eventually the unrest transcended the sphere of domestic politics and radiated throughout the Hellenic world. The end result was that more and more states were drawn into the Athenian orbit through the appeal of democratic Athens to the masses everywhere. Sparta had good reason to fear for the consequences upon its own international position.[22]

A further but perhaps less obvious difficulty in stabilizing the status quo was inherent in the very nature of the dualism between a land and a naval power. A land empire can be an end in itself. Territorial expansionism tends to be directed toward precisely definable goals and will usually reach its outer limits at continental confines. By contrast, a maritime empire, always striving to extend the sway of its power as far as its resources will permit, is less easily contained. Even if the sea itself is sought as an ultimate end, maritime control cannot be secured without the possession of rather widely dispersed territorial bases. Consequently, the aim must be the conquest of diverse land areas well beyond the water's edge. Thus it was only natural that Athenian naval power should have encroached upon the sphere of the Peloponnesians when such infringements promised strategic advantages. Considerations of military security alone seemed to necessitate relentless pressure against the opposing bloc to prevent it from collecting its strength. But economic considerations made it equally important that Athens obtain control of the Gulf of Corinth to secure its export trade, on which it depended not only for its own support but also for maintaining political domination over other states by subjecting their food supply to Athenian control.[23]

Despite its precariousness the balance demonstrated an astonishing durability, though this should not obscure the fact that it might easily have been shattered had one of the adversaries acted without circumspection. We have already spoken of the extraordinarily heightened sensitivity with which the contestants reacted even to minor issues or changes. The general effect of that heightened state of nervousness was to drive both relentlessly to seek improvements in their respective strategic positions. The security of outlying strongholds on which Athens' naval empire rested was always cause for worry. The best way to secure them was to round out the empire by acquiring further naval bases. Such a policy alone could reassure the Athenians that their possessions and their political existence were safe. Sparta too could no longer be content with a static policy. The extension of Athens' maritime control, if it remained unchallenged, would eventually amount to an encirclement and leave Sparta at the mercy of its opponent. The mutual exclusiveness of these goals rendered a more enduring pacification impossible.

The settlement of 446 thus can scarcely be considered more than an armistice [24] during which the struggle continued with changed tactics. Far from being content with its achievements, Athens now attempted to promote its hegemonial designs through bold diplomatic schemes. If Sparta could not be reduced in combat, Athenian policy was far from bankrupt. The hegemony might still be wrested from the opponent through political maneuvers. The most grandiose scheme in the pursuit of such a policy was Pericles' plan for a Panhellenic congress. Though the plan miscarried, it is particularly valuable for the light it sheds on the manifold facets of the political struggle. Invitations were issued to all Hellenes in Europe and Asia to send delegates to Athens to deliberate on the maintenance of peace, the security of the sea, and the common performance of religious duties. Unfortunately the uncertainty of the date—variously given as 448–47 and 446—does not permit us to establish positively Pericles' intent.[25] If the later date were accurate, the project would be a clear indication of Pericles' own skepticism concerning the effectiveness of the recent settlement as the basis for an enduring peace. Such skepticism would seem entirely justified, since there is no reason to assume that by entering into the arrangement Sparta was relinquishing all hope of eventually reducing its rival, or that the Athenians regarded it as anything but a device for enlarging their empire through peaceable means.[26]

The uncertainty of the date leaves the link between the proposed conference and the settlement of 446 within the realm of conjecture. But even if no such connection can be established, the project remains of considerable interest as a full-dress peace offensive, aiming to attain goals different from those it professed. The ostensible aim of securing the peace and the freedom of the sea against the defeated and internally torn Persian empire must immediately arouse suspicion. Taken at face value, the project seems pointless considering the profound political changes that had taken place in Hellas since the expulsion of the Persians. It was also unrealistic in fostering the implied expectation that the anti-Persian wartime alliance could be preserved indefinitely.

What, then, did Pericles hope to accomplish? An answer can perhaps be found in the fragmentary realm of Greek international relations proper.[27] The Peace of Callias had been the source of considerable embarrassment to the Athenians, threatening to disrupt the cohesion of the anti-Persian coalition which was the foundation of the Delian League. It may therefore have appeared useful to conjure up the Persian threat in order to strengthen the solidarity of the Greeks, who had begun to drift apart. But to bring the project more closely in line with changed political conditions, the accent was now on the need for securing the peace rather than on the resumption of the war against the Persians. However, Pericles may well have hoped to accomplish more than a restoration of internal unity. A conference held under Athenian auspices to improve the security of all Greeks could reasonably be expected to entice uncommitted or wavering states to join the Athenian system. If such hopes were to be realized, it was necessary above all to remove suspicions that Athens had expansionist designs. There was no more convincing way to demonstrate good faith than by displaying a disinterested concern for the common cause.

Viewed against the general political background, Pericles' diplomatic maneuver seems clearly aimed at Sparta. No matter how it reacted to the Athenian proposal, Sparta stood to lose political ground. It would have been awkward to participate in a congress held under Athenian auspices, which was an obvious bid for Athenian leadership in defiance of Sparta's traditional claim. It could have done little else but support whatever the Athenians proposed lest it incur the odium of jeopardizing Hellenic unity, thereby contributing to the realization of the rival's ambitions. By declining the invitation Sparta actually frustrated the congress and thus evaded such an embarrassment. Nevertheless, it was caught in an irreducible predicament. Regardless of whether it joined in or whether the congress materialized, Pericles' offensive represented a crushing blow; for in declining the invitation, Sparta left itself open to charges of having thwarted the plan Athens was advancing in the interest of the Panhellenic welfare. Thus, under the pious disguise of promoting the peace, Athens had effectively challenged Sparta's championship of Hellenic freedom. The deeper meaning of the Periclean plan becomes apparent. It was nothing less than an effective weapon in the struggle for hegemony, which had been transferred from the military plane, where a stalemate had been reached, to the more promising political plane.

In spite of the mutual desire to avoid open war and the caution exercised by both sides, three relatively minor incidents finally brought the delicate balance of power to the point of rupture: the Athenian alliance with Corcyra and the incidents concerning Potidaea and Megara. It was the latter that sparked the conflagration. The time had come for Sparta to insist that the breaking point had been reached.

THE "INEVITABILITY" OF WAR

The study of any war sooner or later must focus on its causes and must attempt to ascertain whether it could have been avoided had responsible statesmen been more sober and conciliatory than they were. The human contribution deserves special consideration in our search for the essential features of bipolarism. The story is by no means obvious. We are told by Thucydides that the Spartans were generally slow to go to war except under the pressure of necessity and that they were reluctant to become involved in this particular war.[28] His account also reveals a similar reluctance on the Athenian side during the interval between the conclusion of the treaty of 446 and the outbreak of the war. In addressing his despondent countrymen during the second year of the war, which had brought serious reverses, Pericles even seemed to imply a general dislike for war. As long as there was a real choice, he insisted, war was the "greatest of follies." But where the choice was between war and the loss of independence, war was the only course open to brave men.[29] Although the sincerity of such a statement, made for public consumption, may be open to doubt, it is likely that under these particular circumstances Pericles would have preferred to avoid war if possible. The task of keeping a far-flung empire intact while engaged in an all-out war against a formidable alliance can hardly have been a happy prospect.

Nevertheless, Pericles' contention that the political circumstances of the moment left him no choice cannot be accepted without question. His own contemporaries by and large did not share this view and attributed his uncompromising stand to considerations of a personal nature. But aside from the aspersions that may be cast on Pericles' particular motives, a considerable amount of factual evidence can be marshalled to show that the war was brought on by the willful acts of men. For example, there is little doubt that Athenian policy during the two or three years preceding the outbreak of the war had been provocative and that tensions were heightened to the breaking point through pressures brought to bear upon Sparta by some of its allies, especially Corinth. Thucydides was nevertheless emphatic in contending that Sparta started the war, not because of specific provocations but as the only way out of the impasse into which it had been led by its fear of Athens' growing power. Since the individual incidents causing the outbreak of the war were clearly related to that fear, Thucydides apparently felt that neither side was in a position to make the kind of concessions needed to settle the crisis without surrendering strategic advantages.

Thucydides' interpretation of the causes of the war has often been challenged and has given rise to the charges against him of bias and inaccuracy. Yet it cannot fairly be said that he suppressed evidence of the pressures exerted by Sparta's allies or of Athenian provocations. His narrative shows clearly enough the persistent Corinthian attempts to goad Sparta into action, as well as the part played by the Athenians in the various incidents which precipitated the war. However, his searching analysis did not stop at surface appearances, but tried to distinguish between what caused the war and what occasioned it.[30] It is only natural that the emphasis should have been laid more strongly on the unsolvable predicaments confronting the two powers than on the formal rights and obligations involved in the particular episodes which brought the crisis to a head. In assessing the merits of Thucydides' deterministic interpretation, one should consider briefly the alternative courses that were available to the adversaries.

The stage had been set by the settlement of 446 and the unstable situation created thereby. The surrender of neutral cities to the competitive bidding of both sides was bound to encourage encroachments upon the opponent's sphere of interests and to result in the conclusion of alliances with uncommitted cities which were at war with a member of the opposite camp.[31] Yet, it must be admitted that this seeming weakness of the settlement was also a measure of its realism. To have guaranteed mutual respect for the neutrality of uncommitted cities would have been to neglect the realities of bipolarity. The heightened suspicions provided no grounds for any great confidence in the opponent's respect for such an agreement. The only hope for pacification thus lay in the kind of settlement which the treaty actually provided. But what of the three specific incidents which were directly related to the outbreak of the war? Could the war have been avoided by a greater willingness to settle differences?

The incident concerning Corcyra was the most ominous of the three, for it involved the combination of Athens' fleet with that of another important naval power and thus threatened to upset the military equilibrium. The incident arose from a dispute between Corcyra and its mother-city Corinth. Although the origin of the incident was accidental, its consequences were cataclysmic. It would be unreasonable to say that the Athenians should have denied themselves the advantages inherent in the Corcyrean proposal to combine their respective naval forces. Nevertheless, they were not unmindful of the complications that might result, and it was with reluctance that they accepted the offer, in contravention of the treaty of 446, which might involve them in hostilities with Corinth. Sparta offered its good offices to mediate.[32] However, the Athenians felt that the rejection of the Corcyrean offer would have been more disastrous than a lost battle. The Potidaea episode presents a similarly hopeless picture. Athenian acquiescence in an ally's revolt, abetted and perhaps even instigated by the Corinthians, would have thrown the bipolar balance out of gear and perilously undermined the Athenian position if it were taken to imply admission of weakness.

The most arguable of the three incidents was the decree through which the Athenians excluded the neighboring city of Megara from the ports of the Delian confederacy. Taken at face value, the

of war and of revolts among their subject peoples. Yet by curious irony this self-same fear was remorselessly driving them nearer the abyss. Sparta had good reason to fear that if it continued to ignore Athenian provocations it would find itself reduced to a second-rate position and might even lose its independence. Athens could of course have repealed the Megarian decree and thus postponed the outbreak of the war, but this would probably not have prevented war altogether.[38] Yielding to Spartan pressure in this one instance would not have done away with the rivalry between the two powers which was responsible for the eventual conflagration. Such an action would very likely have been considered an admission of weakness and therefore encouraged further pressure. The general feeling of insecurity which resulted from the precarious military equilibrium was driving both sides to seek supremacy and thus compounding the prevalent fears. As long as both sides were possessed by such fears, peaceful coexistence did not seem a promising solution in the long-run. Eventually the point would be reached where military action would seem the more hopeful course.

If the parties, then, were confronted by an irreducible dilemma, it is impossible to pin the charge of aggression on either. Thucydides evidently was sufficiently aware of the impact of uncontrollable and justified fears to refrain from attempting to do so. Although on the surface Athenian provocations came close to being aggressive, a distinction must be made between aggressive tendencies or an aggressive frame of mind and technical aggression. There is, to be sure, more than a scrap of plausibility in the defense against the repeated charges of aggression which Thucydides puts in the mouth of the Athenians: in accepting an empire that had fallen to them as a result of Sparta's premature withdrawal from the Persian War and in refusing to let it go for reasons of fear, honor, and expediency, they had done no more and no less than what any other power would have done in similar circumstances.[39] By comparison Sparta's declaration of war, based on vague and general charges, appears less than unimpeachable. And yet it must be said in Sparta's favor that a state extending its power without committing military aggression could be as fairly labeled an aggressor as one declaring war or committing the first belligerent act could be considered the guardian of good order. Where the equilibrium has become so precarious as to inflate even minor changes in the distribution of power to a threat of the first magnitude, the question of war guilt loses all meaning; and war, even if sparked off by a seemingly trivial episode, acquires an aura of legitimacy and rationality.

All this is not to say that the political circumstances of the moment had irrevocably closed all avenues to coexistence. It is at least conceivable that Sparta might have effectively contained Athens' power had it been more aggressive politically and tried to undermine Athens' political position. Whether the Spartans ever considered such a course, we do not know. However, Sparta's position as defender of the status quo did not permit it to take any more positive steps toward containing Athens than merely responding to challenges and, if all else failed, going to war. It was the dilemma arising from the inadequacy of a purely responsive policy which, ironically enough, forced the conservative Spartans into the position of technical aggressors.

Theoretically an alternative to the settlement of 446 might have been furnished by a disengagement of the leading powers. Such an arrangement would have presupposed neutralizing crisis areas and guaranteeing the integrity of uncommitted states, instead of leaving them to mutual competitive bidding. However, Thucydides' account inspires little confidence in the possibility of such a solution. What stands out is that the Big Two had in fact been quite impatient with neutrals ever since the Persian War and were becoming increasingly so as the bipolar mold hardened. At the outbreak of the Peloponnesian War, neutrals seem largely to have evaporated, and residues of neutrality were progressively eliminated during the war.

The political facts of the moment, then, stubbornly resisted an easing of the situation. There seemed to be no formula available that could lead out of the bipolar impasse. The interplay of political forces had attained such vehemence as to elude the control of the leading powers. To stress this loss of freedom of action is not to imply the presence of metaphysical necessity. It is merely to say that political developments had come to such a pass as to force statesmen into war if their countries' political independence was to be preserved. This seems to be the basis of Pericles' view that war had become a necessity.[40]

Such an interpretation is likely to encounter objections. Historians have often rejected, in general and with reference to this particular war, the assumption of inevitability, insisting that not even the consideration of balance of power can eliminate the possibility of choice. Historical examples are frequently cited to show that even where the distribution of power threatened the security of nations, wars have still been the result of free choice among a number of available alternatives. There is much merit in such arguments, but they need to be qualified. Most of the evidence such critics have marshalled refers to incidents within the context of widely diffused power. Events must be judged differently in a bipolar context. The bipolar system is constantly in danger of becoming monocentric and the threat of a power monopoly keeps the world in perpetual fear since there is little hope that such power can be resisted or restrained. The core issue of the bipolar struggle therefore is not the protection of vested interests, but the prevention of a worldwide tyranny in order to insure survival in a tolerable measure of independence. Stated in the broadest terms, reconciliation here was precluded by the fear that any surrender of position might ultimately lead to total and perpetual enslavement. In the narrower sense, Athens' security was contingent upon the integrity of its empire, while Sparta felt an equally strong need to redress of the balance of power which Athens' growing power had disturbed beyond toleration.

Such considerations do not necessarily force us to conclude that there was nothing Sparta could have done at any juncture. As leader of the wartime coalition against Persia it might well have taken timely measures to checkmate the rise of so formidable a rival as Athens. But once the threshold of bipolarity was reached, events had passed the point at which peace could have been preserved indefinitely through settlements.

Tactical aspects

The effect of bipolarity upon the war itself was more sweeping than one might suppose. The bearing which the distribution of power had on the ends sought by the belligerents can hardly escape notice. In the decades following the Persian War the Athenians, in search of wealth and glory, were little inclined to acknowledge the need for more restraint than was demanded by ordinary prudence; but their desire for self-gratification was far less pronounced when the Peloponnesian War began. The overriding issue now was survival. This goal was considerably more modest than the earlier expansionism, but unfortunately it was largely intangible and ambiguous in its practical details. Neither Athens, rising in defense of its empire, nor Sparta, driven to assert its military supremacy, was initially bent on the total destruction of the enemy, even though total destruction may have seemed necessary for obtaining a clear-cut decision. Sparta's moderation in particular is manifest in its continued willingness to settle short of war, even after the initial attack had taken place.[41] Reasons of the balance of power may have been a factor since Athens was an effective counterpoise to the ambitions of Corinth and Thebes.[42] But it is doubtful that such calculations would have been of great consequence in the first flush of the war had not the political temper generally been one of restraint.

Despite the moderate initial goals of insuring independence and securing possessions, it was not easy to reduce the war aims to specifics as the fighting progressed. The actual conduct of the war presents a picture considerably different from what had been intended.[43] Signs of total warfare can early be observed, perhaps not so much in the modern sense of impressing entire populations into combat but in the intent of totally reducing the enemy in the field and at home through any and all means available. Odd as it may seem, Sparta was first to employ the methods of total war. By periodically invading Attica and devastating the countryside, it virtually destroyed for a generation the area's economic basis, which consisted largely of olive crops requiring close to thirty years for a commercial yield. The same cynicism which was implied in condemning an entire generation to starvation later led the Athenians to interfere in Sicilian affairs. The request of Leontini for aid against Syracuse was too tempting an opportunity to miss, inasmuch as the conquest of Sicily would enable Athens to cut off the grain supply of the Peloponnesians.[44] The well-known outrages against the populations of Plataea, Mytilene, Melos, Scione, Torone, and Mycalessus are further evidence of the use of total war methods.

The racial and ethnic kinship of the belligerent peoples did nothing to diminish the ferocity of war; rather it seems to have heightened the intensity of what in effect was an internecine war. The fratricidal nature of the war was accentuated by the factional strife between the oligarchs and the masses, which had simultaneously come to a head in many cities and was spreading internal revolutions and violence throughout the battling confederacies.[45]

In the realm of military estimates, the bipolar equilibrium created a difficult problem. The complete unpredictability of the outcome of the war caused both sides, once the die was cast, to tackle the job with rare vigor and self-assurance. All factors considered, the Athenian prospects appeared more favorable. The possession of an unrivaled navy, immense actual and potential monetary resources, and extraordinary ingenuity and flexibility gave them an unquestionable advantage over the opponent.[46] It was impossible to foresee that the tide would turn, especially as it was not so much Sparta's own strength that was responsible as it was the receipt of last-minute Persian financial aid which enabled Sparta to build a navy capable of successfully challenging that of the Athenians. Sparta's cause was further aided by Athenian misfortunes and blunders. The plague in the second year of the war, which among other calamities claimed Pericles' life, certainly could not have been included in the calculations of even the most astute statesmen. As for the ability of the Athenians to cope with the problem of financial over-extension (resulting from the dole and from public works projects to alleviate discontent and check moral degradation), it was at best possible to venture a guess.

Athens' initial advantage was buttressed by the peculiarity of the current bipolar system which divided the two camps according to the arm in which each excelled. No Iron Curtain established clearly defined territorial lines; rather, the line of demarcation followed the division between land and sea. Initially the superiority of each side in its favored arm led to a mutual avoidance of the theater in which the opponent was at home.[47] It may have seemed for a while that the functional division might be permanent, since financial limitations prevented the Peloponnesians from entering into naval competition and the Athenians from incurring the additional expense of developing a land army comparable to Sparta's.

Actually there was little reason why Athens should have wanted to create a land force of such magnitude. Its navy was safe from land-bound forces, and there was little basis for fear that a perpetual stalemate would result. Possessing the more modern arm and having a wider radius of action,[48] Athens very likely would be able to cut the Peloponnesians off from the sources of their food supply while insuring its own. Its extraordinary mobility also enabled Athens to control overseas allies and devastate enemy territory without being subject to retaliation. Pericles was fully conscious of the unique advantages of the Athenian position. Their position, he told his compatriots, was that of islanders, it was impregnable. The desolation of Attica would not do them any serious harm if only they did not let themselves become involved in land battles. And to underscore the limited value of territorial possessions for a naval power he would have advocated, if he could have, the immediate adoption of a scorched earth policy.[49] Although Pericles may have been willing to go further than many of his predecessors in exploiting the advantages of maritime position, he was not the first to recognize them. Long before him Themistocles had revealed an astute awareness of his city's unique position when he transferred the Athenian population to Salamis in the Persian War. Evidently, the lesson of Salamis had not been wasted on Pericles.[50]

Sparta's position was considerably more difficult. If it was to avoid an effective Athenian naval blockade, it could not rely solely on familiar arms and methods; sooner or later it would have to build a navy superior to that of Athens.[51] Since this was an unpleasant prospect for many reasons, the decision to do so was deferred as long as possible. This may explain the inadequacy of Sparta's strategy during the early phase of the war, which consisted almost exclusively of repeated invasions of Attica. But even later in the war when the superiority of the naval arm was generally acknowledged, the entrenchment of its forces at Decelea in Attica, though of dubious utility, still remained the cornerstone of Sparta's strategy.[52] Even at that late date Sparta seemed to ignore what was obvious to all the insular peoples, that is, that a decision could be had only on the sea.[53]

Subsequent developments clearly show that the outcome of the war depended above all on the Peloponnesians' ability to defeat, or in any event resist, the Athenian navy, rather than on the accomplishments of Sparta's land forces. In the end, Sparta had no alternative but to yield to the demands of the changed technology of warfare. But it did so only after the Athenians had suffered a disastrous defeat in Sicily. The annihilation of the Athenian expeditionary force represented the turning point in the war for two reasons: the Athenian ambition to establish world dominion had at last been openly revealed, inevitably heightening Sparta's anxiety; and, the impact of the shock was reinforced by the fact that the equilibrium had been decisively upset for the first time.[54] The success of the Sicilians in challenging Athens' naval supremacy and the reverberations this was causing throughout the empire gave the Spartans reason to hope that the war could be terminated quickly if only they made the necessary effort. It was in face of such hopes and fears that the Peloponnesians finally tackled the job of building a first-rate fleet.[55]

If the actual course of events thus upset the optimistic expectations which the Athenians had rightfully entertained at the outset and which were shared by some of the more cautious Spartans, the explanation is to be found in the political rather than in the military or economic realm. Driven on by their energy and ambition and encouraged by successes, the Athenians often found it difficult to practice the degree of moderation needed for a responsible exercise of their great power.[56] Time and again they courted disaster by yielding to the temptation to overextend themselves. The most dramatic illustration was the Sicilian expedition between 415 and 413. Regardless of the plan's merits, the involvement with another first-rate democratic naval power such as Syracuse was extraordinarily risky and required prudent planning as well as utmost discipline in the execution.

What enabled Athens to hold out as long as it did against all odds resulting from frequently reckless actions was an unusual recuperative ability, most impressively displayed in its comeback after the fiasco in Sicily.[57] But even its immense resources and resourcefulness could not indefinitely bear the strain of periodically rebuilding the fleet from scratch. Eventually Athens' naval power was to lose its force and efficiency. The immediate reasons were succinctly stated by Nicias, the Athenian general in command of the Sicilian expedition: the navy had lost its original skill; foreign seamen were being drained off by the opponent's competitive bidding; and the natural lack of docility of Athenian crews made for poor discipline.[58] A more potent reason perhaps was that Athenian finances eventually reached the point of exhaustion[59] at a time when Sparta's monetary resources were being liberally replenished by the Persian king.[60] Under such adverse conditions Athenian seamanship eventually had to yield the first place to Sparta.

Another point of interest related to the bipolar system is the location of the theaters of war. It is a truism that battles are fought where they can be fought. But this observation must be qualified to the effect that battles are fought where a decision can be obtained. Where a dividing line exists between two clearly defined opposing camps, attention is focused upon the adjacent areas on either side; and these areas are most jealously guarded against encroachments. Frequently changes are made more easily in remote areas. However, an equally important consideration in developing strategic plans is the respective military specialty of the opposing parties. To begin with, Athens' interest seems to have been focused on areas close to the center, that is, the mainland and particularly the coastal regions. But in the long-run such a strategy would have required a first-rate land force. It was cheaper and more effective to blockade the Peloponnesians and starve them out. This was a task which the Athenians with their great navy and their naval experience could safely attempt. It was the wide radius of Athenian naval action, carrying operations further away from the center of the power system, that ultimately forced the Spartans to adapt themselves to the arm of their enemy. Although the Peloponnesian War was fought in many different areas, the peripheral areas turned out to be of decisive importance.[61]

When the Spartans were finally ready to build a navy with which to attack Athens where it was most vulnerable, the shift of the theater of operations to peripheral areas begins to become a definite pattern. Evidently an attack upon the city proper promised little success if the Athenians abandoned it, as Pericles had counseled them to do, and carried on the war from their ships. True, signs of a trend toward the periphery had already appeared in the early war years. The very incidents setting off the conflagration involved the cities of Potidaea and Epidamnus, which were both located on the fringes of the Hellenic world. With the outbreak of the war both sides immediately turned their attention to peripheral areas by quickly appealing to the Persian king and other barbarians for help.[62] The Athenians also considered it worth their while to send settlers to Potidaea [63] and almost lost their balance over the defection of distant Mytilene.[64] As early as 427–26 we see the Athenians involved in operations in Sicily,[65] attempting to break the stalemate reached in the war.[66] An event of major importance was the conquest of Amphipolis by Sparta in 423, for the first time driving a wedge into the Athenian empire.[67] Nevertheless, during the Archidamian War the heavy core of the fighting still remained concentrated on the mainland and adjacent waters with the result that no decisive success could be scored anywhere. During the Peace of Nicias peripheral areas began to receive more conscious attention for the obvious reason that both sides, constrained by the peace not to invade each other's territory, found convenient fields of activity abroad.[68] But it was only with the Sicilian disaster, when the naval power appeared so weakened as to invite a showdown in its own theater, that the shift of operations to the periphery became a major factor in overall strategy.

With the construction of a navy by Sparta, the bipolar balance underwent a fundamental change. The dividing line between the land power and the sea power now became blurred. The year 412, when Sparta was first equipped with a sizable navy, saw no major action on the mainland; but it was notable for the mass defections of Athenian allies in Ionia, which received encouragement from Sparta.[69] In view of Athens' ability to obtain food supplies from the East, the main theater of war was shifted in that direction in 411, and the Hellespont became the focus of attention for both parties.[70] From 412 to 405 practically all the fighting was centered about the Hellespont and the Bosporus,[71] and it was in Asia that the final decision fell. Athens' dependence on food supplies from the Black Sea, the collapse of its empire in that area through revolts of its subjects, as well as the decisive influence of Persian intervention, all combine to explain the paramount importance of peripheral areas. After the defeat suffered at Aegospotami the concerted Spartan actions against Athens by land and in blockading Piraeus could no longer be resisted.[72]

Political aspects: unconditional surrender or peace?

The war was a disaster of the first magnitude both because of the sufferings it inflicted on the Greeks and because it was leading the Greek city-states into certain decline. The extent of the misfortune makes us pause to wonder whether the pursuit of the war until one of the belligerents had been forced into submission was the only way to end the conflict or whether a negotiated settlement might not have been a practical alternative once the opponents had demonstrated their virtual invincibility. The termination of the war through other than military means no doubt would have been universally welcomed in view of the extraordinary cruelty accompanying the internecine war.[73] The belligerents themselves, fearful of the uncertain end result, showed little enthusiasm for the war. Circumstances thus seemed auspicious for a negotiated settlement.

And yet, the matter was not as simple as it appears. The most ardent commitment to reason cannot dispose of the fact that wars of extended duration are never fought in an atmosphere of cold rationality which would permit a sober disentanglement of the issues, however desirable and even necessary this may appear from a more distant vantage point.

The Peloponnesian War in particular had created an emotion-charged atmosphere, as the cruel treatment of the Plataeans at the hands of the Spartans and the death sentence imposed upon the people of Mytilene by the Athenians (repealed only at the last moment) seem to suggest. Nor does Pericles' last speech in the second year of the war, as related by Thucydides, contain any hint that he envisaged any other possibility than the decisive defeat of the enemy.[74] But at the bottom, there were more compelling reasons for the apparent unwillingness to settle short of the adversary's unconditional surrender. The same conditions which had thwarted the prewar attempts at peaceful coexistence still prevailed. They were neither of Pericles' nor of anybody else's making but were inherent in the nature of the distribution of power proper. The fear of a monocentric universe which had been responsible for the breakdown of the peace in 431 was now effectively preventing a settlement of the war.

Here, then, was another peculiarity of the bipolar war. In a multiple power system, wars are frequently settled short of the total defeat of one of the belligerents. But even when they are fought until one side surrenders unconditionally, the immediate and almost automatic realignment of the major powers normally insures that a victory is not total and that no one power emerges as the sole ruler of the universe. The bipolar system provided no such corrective. Consequently, neither side was likely to surrender positions that might give the opponent the edge needed to become a power monopolist or to stop fighting before being assured that the adversary's power was destroyed beyond the possibility of resurrection. It seems therefore reasonable to suppose that the contestants could perceive no other possibilities to avert that frightening prospect than to keep on fighting to secure the total defeat of the opponent.

Thucydides' story shows that peace feelers were repeatedly extended and that numerous opportunities to make a settlement were missed. It would, no doubt, be easiest to be content with noting the shortcomings of individual men and bringing accusations against them. But the persistence of obstacles which cannot be attributed to the prejudices of the personalities entrusted with the conduct of affairs suggest more basic difficulties than ill-intentioned or inept statesmanship. Obviously, offers of settlement invariably emanated from the side that had suffered reverses, and this was their main weakness. The best such offers would normally concede was the restoration of the status quo, and that was small inducement to the side that for the moment had the upper hand. A more interesting possibility would have been an alliance establishing a joint Atheno-Spartan hegemony over the Greek states. Such an arrangement was actually offered by Sparta in 425 in return for lifting the siege of the island of Sphacteria off the southwestern tip of the Peloponnese.[75] However, the Athenians, having just won a success, were out for more ambitious gains than the status quo plus an alliance. A peace offer based on the status quo was again made by Sparta in 410, but in view of recent successes in the Hellespont it was rejected by Alcibiades and his radical party.[76] Another offer on the same terms was made in 406 after the battle of Arginusae, but the radical party then in control in Athens again rejected it.[77] Athens in turn sued for peace in the second year of the war when it had reached the lowest point of despair as a result of the plague, but this time its overtures were rejected by Sparta.[78]

The rejection of a joint hegemony must have been frustrating to many Greeks. Here seemed to be an opportunity to end the horrors of war without creating a power monopoly. And yet it is doubtful that the plan would have worked even if the Athenians had been more receptive. A hint as to the prospects of such an agreement may be gleaned from the arrangements which were actually made along similar lines a few years later. The so-called Peace of Nicias of the year 421 was followed by an alliance to in-

sure compliance with the terms of the peace by Sparta's Peloponnesian allies.[79] Despite its seven years' duration, the scheme was
far from a success, and signs of belligerency appeared soon. Although the fighting had stopped, fears and tensions had not sub-
sided, and more or less concealed warfare continued on the
periphery.[80] The plan's failure was not altogether accidental and
had in fact been anticipated by its architect, the moderate Nicias
who in spite of his desire for peace looked upon it merely as a
temporary expedient.[81]

Theoretically it would have been entirely possible for Athens
to accept the peace as a long-term arrangement. Implying not only
de jure recognition by Sparta of almost all its imperial possessions
but also a *de facto* acknowledgment of the empire's indestruc-
tibility, it represented a major triumph.[82] Yet there were sufficiently
obstinate obstructions to a lasting settlement. Alcibiades' personal
ambitions certainly did not bode well for sustained cooperation
in the supra-national enterprise of restoring order to Hellas.[83]
But even if he had been more moderate, it is doubtful that the aggressive temper of the Athenian masses could have been contained
by a mere treaty, inasmuch as the favorable terms of the peace
were bound to create an optimistic inclination toward further
gains.

For Sparta the peace could only be a source of embarrassment.
Having failed to establish its military superiority, it was now revealing the vacuity of its promise to liberate the Hellenic world
from the Athenian threat. The arrangement must therefore have
appeared to Sparta, as evidently it did to many Hellenes, the equiv-
alent of a major political defeat. Sparta's embarrassment was
further aggravated by the loss of control over many of its allies,
who felt betrayed by the treaty that had been concluded in their
behalf.[84] The lack of enthusiasm among such unwilling parties
endangered the peace from the very outset. The alliance with
Athens could hardly be considered adequate compensation for
the loss of prestige and of allied support. Coercion of recalcitrant
allies alone was a ticklish matter under the given conditions, since
it could cause widespread resentment throughout the Spartan camp.

But to invoke Athenian aid against the allies would have meant a total abdication of Sparta's already shaky hegemony.[85]

The main weakness of the alliance was a lack of fundamental unity between the partners. An equilibrium of power was hardly enough to sustain a joint hegemony which depended for its proper functioning on mutual cooperation. No mere contractual arrangement could eradicate the mutual suspicion sufficiently to insure strict observance of the treaty provisions against the resistance of friends and allies. Concern for its security therefore did not permit Sparta to neglect considerations of long-range strategy. A realistic appraisal showed the improbability of a dynamic maritime power such as Athens being deterred either through agreement or a temporary military stalemate. Even if it was reasonably well-intentioned, fear of the Peloponnesians and even more of its imperial subjects were sufficient reasons for making the pursuit of eventual domination of the Hellenic world appear a vital necessity. There are indications that thoughts of this nature were actually looming large in Athenian thinking. According to Thucydides, the Sicilian leader Hermocrates charged,[86] and Alcibiades in fact confessed,[87] that the Athenian design was to dominate the entire surrounding world. The alarming aspects of Athens' naval supremacy also extended into the economic realm. Lacking in economic self-sufficiency[88] Sparta would have been ill-advised to perpetuate an arrangement which left its means of subsistence at the mercy of its rival. Sparta's apprehensions of Athenian designs were fully vindicated by the aggression against the island Melos and against Sicily. There seemed to remain no other way out of these straits than to break Athens' naval monopoly.

Perhaps the chief reason that all arrangements to end the war were doomed was the lack of a balancer. There was small chance that such a force could be called into being under the bipolar distribution of power, characterized as it was by the evaporation of all powers of sufficient consequence to play that part. The maintenance of the rough equilibrium on which their continued independence rested therefore was the sole responsibility of the Big

Two. Hence the irrepressible fear and suspicion, the rigidity and the nervousness of their policies.

The creation of a "third force" was nevertheless attempted against all odds during the Peace of Nicias.[89] Frightened by the apparent harmony between Athens and Sparta, Corinth succeeded in persuading Argos to undertake the task of forming an independent force with genuine freedom of action.[90] But was it realistic to expect that such an effort could succeed? Was there any chance that Argos' alliance could be a match for the combined power of Athens and Sparta? Initially the prospects may not have seemed entirely unpromising, especially if Boeotia had joined the independent Peloponnesian alliance; but the preponderant power of the Atheno-Spartan combination was to bring the enterprise to naught.[91] Even if the attempt had succeeded, it is doubtful that the bipolar pattern would have been displaced by some other configuration. The more likely result would have been a new bipolar balance, either with the Atheno-Spartan bloc on one side and the "third force" on the other, or with one of the Big Two joining the "third force." However, the more natural course was the return of the Peloponnesian allies into the Spartan fold as soon as it became clear that the joint Atheno-Spartan hegemony held out little promise of being effective and enduring.[92]

A balancer finally appeared on the stage in 412 when the Spartan treaty with the Persian king made him the virtual arbiter of Hellenic politics.[93] Unfortunately for Greece, the Persian king was hardly the kind of balancer who was interested in a decision and the restoration of peace and order. On the contrary, he used his position to perpetuate rather than liquidate the bipolar balance and the war. Only when the power of Athens in a last effort once again assumed threatening proportions did he reluctantly help to bring about a decision by giving his unequivocal support to the Peloponnesians.

chapter 4

SUPERPOWERS
AND OTHERS

ALLIES

The part played by the lesser sovereignties in the bipolar contest deserves special consideration. The overwhelming military strength of the two leading powers presumably should have reduced them to a position of no great consequence, but all the evidence is against such an assumption. The policies of both the Athenians and the Spartans revealed a lively concern for their allies, and the competition for the friendship of uncommitted states clearly occupied a prominent place in their respective political strategies. During the "cold war" and the subsequent open war, efforts to break up the opposing alliance and to integrate the fragments into their own had top priority rating in the planning of both sides.

The value of alliances

Despite the seeming paradox, this concern is easy to explain. It is a truism that strong and dynamic states normally strive to extend their control over others. But oddly enough the drive seems especially pronounced in the bipolar world where it virtually turns into a law of existence. Such tendencies are frequently attributed to emotional causes. Yet this view fails to take into account that, irrespective of the unique military strength of Athens and Sparta, the addition of third states to one or the other side might be de-

cisive in a war between two more or less evenly matched powers.
Many references can be found in Thucydides' account—both in
the form of direct observations and of statements put in the mouth
of the participants—to show that neither side could or believed it
could "go it alone" and to point up the ineptness of an isolationist
policy for a major power in an inchoate as well as in a fully articu-
lated bipolar situation.[1]

A few specific instances may be cited for the light they shed
on the reasons for the superpowers' interest in their allies. Even
before the outbreak of open war the Spartan king Archidamus
made an issue of the indispensability of allies for Sparta's security.[2] The accuracy of his forecast was later confirmed when the
Spartan general Brasidas unequivocally admitted in the midst of
the war that Sparta had miscalculated if it expected to defeat the
Athenians single-handedly.[3] The interest of the Athenians in their
allies had similar grounds. Their concern over the defection of
Mytilene had its rationale in the fear that the island of Lesbos,
with its sizable fleet and extensive resources, might join their
enemies.[4] And we are told that they concluded the armistice of
423 in order to halt a widespread allied revolt.[5] For much the
same reasons the Ionian exiles accompanying Sparta's delayed
rescue mission to Lesbos in 427 counseled that no effort be spared
to encourage the defection of Athens' allies, since Athens depended
for the defense of its empire on the revenue and strategic positions
which they provided.[6]

The chief incentive for the Athenians to conclude the Peace
of Nicias probably had a similar basis.[7] It is also interesting to
note that in their distress after the Sicilian disaster the Athenians
dipped deep into their badly depleted finances to prevent the defection of Chios.[8] Among the various incentives economic ones
no doubt loomed large, and they assumed an especially great importance for a naval power. It was probably no mere accident that
Sparta's decision to follow the Athenian example of collecting
monetary contributions from the allies was made at the time when
it undertook to build a fleet.[9]

The strategic value of adding bases, revenue, soldiers, and war materials does not tell the whole story. The vital need to keep such assets out of the enemy's reach provided an equally strong incentive. But whatever the reasons, it is clear that allies were considered to be of crucial importance. In fact, it was precisely because the Athenians refused to relinquish control of their allies that Sparta started the war.[10]

The changing nature of alliances

The pattern of allied relations during the prewar period and the war years suggests a close correspondence between the hardening dualism of power and the evaporation of the allies' freedom of international action. The connection is especially apparent in the Athenian system. As has been seen, the Athenians progressively tightened their control over what initially was a voluntary alliance of formally equal partners through military coercion and confederate political institutions. Although centralizing tendencies had been present from the beginning, it was not until Athens put its foreign policy on a clearly anti-Spartan course that the allies were reduced to the status of virtual satellites.

The harsh methods employed to maintain Athenian supremacy could not fail to arouse resentment and to cause allied resistance. Although the allies by and large had a good case, a few points can nevertheless be made for the Athenian position. It is by no means certain that the deviation of the *de facto* distribution of power in the league from the formal constitutional pattern was occasioned by sinister designs. Even in the absence of any conscious intent Athens would necessarily have risen to a dominant position in the league as a result of the growing disparity between its power and that of the allies.[11] It must also be admitted that the demands for loyalty and support from the allies were not an unreasonable return for the protection promised them, nor were these demands peculiar to the Delian League. It would be equally difficult to maintain that it was a sign of marked dishonesty when the Athenians incorporated their allies' pecuniary contributions into their treasury and used the common funds for purposes of their own so long as they lived up to the obligation to provide for the common defense.[12] What was unreasonable was the severity with which they exacted performance of the allies' obligations, and it was this which earned them the reputation of having enslaved their fellow Greeks.

As for the allies, they were not easily convinced of the merit of the Athenian position and refused to accept Athenian domination as legitimate. No doubt the Athenians could have minimized resentment by using a formula more congenial to men of the independent Greek spirit. For example, a durable bond of union might have been forged by extending Athenian citizenship to the citizens of allied states.[13] From such a shared citizenship a genuine common sense might have emerged in place of the tenuous and ephemeral stability resting on terror.[14] In view of the migration to Athens of thousands of persons from allied states, who were anxious to take advantage of the many attractions Athens had to offer,[15] a liberal nationality policy very likely would have produced beneficial effects. However, the Athenians remained indifferent to the need of maintaining even the appearance of a partnership at a time when substantive domination had already been substituted for consent, and they continued to restrict citizenship to those entitled to it by birth.[16] The reason was probably not bigotry pure and simple, but a justified concern over the effects of an enlarged citizenry upon the domestic power structure. The balance between populist and oligarchic forces in Athens was precarious and could easily have been upset if the majority of newly admitted citizens inclined toward oligarchy. But however valid such considerations may have been, this failure to take the allies into a genuine partnership in a more tightly organized confederacy seriously aggravated an already difficult situation.

Athenian practices received then and have since received severe moral condemnation and have frequently been contrasted with Sparta's more enlightened policy toward its allies. The available evidence certainly seems to suggest a less oppressive relationship within the Spartan system. It is impossible to ignore the liberal implications of Sparta's public commitment to protect the autonomy of the Greek states or to belittle the seriousness of the purpose for which it went to war. Its liberality is also reflected in the institutional arrangements within its league which seemed to insure some measure of formal independence. Most important was the retention by the allied assembly of the power to make decisions binding upon the members.[17]

Doubts must nevertheless arise concerning the nature of the substantive relations between Sparta and its allies in view of strategic exigencies of the moment. It was no less urgent for the Spartans than for the Athenians to exercise effective control over their alliance system. Stemming the Athenian tide was a more ambitious task than they could expect to accomplish alone and required the combined effort of the entire league. There remains therefore some doubt as to whether the appearance of a relationship based purely on consent had any basis in political reality. The fact that institutional forms often conceal rather than reveal the actual distribution of power is well known. It will therefore be necessary to take a closer look at the league headed by Sparta, with particular attention to the degree of autonomy which it actually allowed its members.

The record is far from adequate to permit any very definite deductions. But there is enough evidence to justify substantial doubt that matters within the Spartan system were all that was claimed. Even on the surface there are good indications that Sparta was not prepared to relinquish its supremacy over its allies and in fact had devised effective methods to secure it. Sparta's allies, like Athens', were pledged not to secede from the league.[18] The practice of dispatching supervisory officers (*xenagoi*) to allied cities was well established. During the first part of the war, in 423, Sparta violated the principle of autonomy outright by appointing governors (*harmostai*) over various cities in disregard of the guarantees it had given.[19] Not unlike Athens, it showed considerable concern for the constitutional forms prevailing in allied cities and, where these differed from its own, endeavored as far as possible to effect a change. Nor did Sparta insist any less emphatically than its opponent on the punctilious discharge of military and pecuniary obligations, which were enforced by its supervisory officers in allied cities.[20] Similarities can also be seen in the making of policy, which in substance was as much the practical prerogative of the *hegemon* in the Peloponnesian as in the Delian confederacy. In this connection it is of interest to note that none of the treaties Sparta concluded with the Persian king later in the war contain provisions for ratification by the allies.[21] Even if strategic considerations occasionally made it appear advisable to concede to an ally an impressive degree of formal independence, conformity was normally exacted in the end.

A number of specific episodes are related by Thucydides to suggest that in important matters the formal participation of the allies in making decisions frequently was little more than a sham. This may well have been true of the deliberations preceding the commencement of the war. Although the allies were consulted on the propriety and advisability of making war against Athens,[22] they were not convened to consider the matter until after the Spartan assembly had cast its vote in favor of war,[23] the act that decided the issue. A more glaring departure from the principle of consent was the conclusion of the alliance with Athens (following the Peace of Nicias) which Sparta made without consulting its allies.[24] The high-handed procedure caused bitter resentment and actually sparked off an open revolt against the hegemonial city. Sparta did not remain indifferent in the face of such threats to its league's cohesion and maintained its position with military force when necessary.[25] Nor was Sparta above forcible intervention in the affairs of Peloponnesian states;[26] and some of the Peloponnesians, especially the Mantineans, clearly regarded their status in the League as one of enslavement.[27] Perhaps the clearest indication of the dependent status of Sparta's allies is Pericles' retort after receiving Sparta's ultimatum immediately preceding the outbreak of the war—that Athens would respect the autonomy of Greek states if Sparta did likewise.[28]

It would of course be idle to deny that at the acme of Athenian power the two blocs did show differences in their internal distribution of power. However, when the substantive relations between the two superpowers and their respective allies are compared, the difference turns out to be largely one of degree. The two systems resembled each other in "constitutional" basis and structure— resting as they both did on treaties mostly entered into voluntarily —and there also did not seem to be any marked difference in the determination of the leading powers to maintain and strengthen internal unity. When the chips were down, Sparta would provide effective guidance and assert its final authority in making policy for the Peloponnesian League. Although it had been slow to tighten its control in response to the new problems arising from changed political circumstances, it eventually succeeded in building an offensive and defensive alliance which was no less effective than that of the Athenians. In fact, in preparation for the great showdown, both alliance systems went through a similar evolution in the course of which the hegemonial powers virtually reduced their allies to the status of dependent communities. As the showdown approached and power alignments took shape, the line between empire and alliance became increasingly blurred on both sides and eventually the Spartan and the Athenian alliances became empires in fact.

The political conditions of the period provide ample explanation for the growing illiberality of hegemonial relations. Since the intimate connection between the progressive bipolarization of power and the rise of *de facto* empires stands out more clearly in the case of the Delian than of the Peloponnesian League, it seems useful to take a closer look at the causes of the change within the Athenian alliance. Unfortunately the moment of transition from hegemonial leadership to imperial rule is difficult to pinpoint inasmuch as the hegemonial form of organization persisted even after reciprocity had given way to domination. The persistence of a formal structure at variance with the changed internal distribution of power can be explained by the fact that empire as a political form was not known to the Greeks. Dependent status did not commonly take the form of territorial rule of one state over another, but consisted in the subjection to *de facto* domination unaccompanied by the assumption of formal jurisdiction on the part of the superior power. In fact, the Greeks did not even have a word for imperialism in their language. The term *arche,* used to denote imperialist relations, did not originally mean anything very different from *hegemonia,* and both terms were frequently used interchangeably.[29]

The contention that the Delian League was an imperial organization from the outset, as evidenced by the appointment of Athenian tax collectors (*hellenotamiai*), can be safely dismissed. A rationalized procedure for monetary collections is perfectly normal to any defensive league and does not by itself prove the existence of an oppressive relationship. The two specific events which have frequently been considered turning points, the transfer of the confederate treasury to Athens in 454 and the Athenian peace with Persia of 449, are not entirely convincing either. No doubt the transfer of the treasury reflected a change in Athens' position within the league and probably contributed more than any other event to the allies' agitation. However, the very fact of the transfer, whatever its reasons, was an unmistakable symbol of the already existing Athenian domination, which is all the more apparent in view of the general acquiescence of the allies to a move that could not possibly have been universally regarded with equanimity. The year 454 thus seems too late a date for the transition; this also rules out the Peace of Callias as the turning point. It is more likely that the transition occurred gradually and that the increase in tribute, the transfer of the treasury, and the denial of the right of secession together indicate a *de facto* change which must have taken place some time before 454.

The transition no doubt was accelerated by the restlessness of the Athenians. But to dismiss their imperialism as an expression of their "national character" is too simple. The view that Athenian imperialism was motivated by economic considerations has more to commend it. An empire ready to be mulcted through tributes certainly must have been of enormous importance for the conduct of the war. Nor is it possible to ignore the powerful impetus which derived from the economic needs of the poor classes.[30] However, the relevance of economic explanations does not *per se* prove either that economic motives were the only ones or that they were of greater consequence than political factors.[31] The foundations of the empire had in fact been laid at a time and under circumstances when economic considerations carried little weight; and even when they gained in importance, they remained subservient to political ends.[32]

In reducing the allies to the status of economic dependencies and practically forcing them to beg for admission to the imperial system for reasons of economic survival—notwithstanding the political submission which membership implied—Athens had prepared the ground for economic exploitation and political control over subject allies.[33] Economic pressures were employed chiefly as a simple and effective method of building an empire and only secondarily as a means of increasing wealth. The more ambitious expansive designs of the Athenians, such as the conquest of the island of Melos and the plans to conquer Sicily, Italy, and Carthage, were not primarily motivated by the desire for economic gain.[34] It should also be added that the aims of Athenian imperialism were neither as limited nor as specific as the economic argument seems to imply.

There are a number of reasons—psychological and military, personal and political—for the imperialistic trend. The conversion of the Delian League into an empire, prepared for by the actions of Themistocles, Aristides, and Cimon, and completed by Pericles, might suggest personal ambition as the ultimate cause. And ambition may have played a part, but there were tactical and psychological factors which would have prevented a more tolerant attitude toward disloyal allies. On the tactical side, the allies were deluding themselves if they regarded the Persian threat as conclusively eliminated with the Athenian victory at the Eurymedon River. The Athenian protectorate continued to provide the only effective insurance against future Persian attacks. The same consideration applies to the Peace of Callias, the effectiveness of which depended on the existence of a strong Athenian fleet ready at any time to be interposed between the Greeks and the Persians.[35] From the psychological perspective, it was equally unrealistic to expect a dynamic power such as Athens to relinquish—out of respect for an abstract legalism—the dominion which the inertia of the allies had permitted it to establish.[36] The hardships and sacrifices suffered in defending the allies' security when the Persian threat was acute precluded a sudden dismissal of the erstwhile protector when the danger seemed remote. It is therefore little wonder that the Athenians should have met allied resistance with determination. Voluntary cooperation had to give way to force, which did not stop short of interference with the allies' internal affairs.

Such psychological and military considerations no doubt carried much weight, but they neither seem to have much relevance to a policy that was chiefly directed against Sparta nor do they explain why no alternatives to imperialism were seriously proposed in the discussions of the Athenians. In view of the deep cleavages between the contending factions it seems strange that few Athenians apparently were prepared to challenge the desirability of the imperialistic policy.[37] To be sure, differences of opinion existed between extremists and moderates as to whether their city's policy should be aimed at supremacy in Hellas or the continuation of a dual hegemony at home, with expansion at the expense of the Persian king.[38] Athens' policy oscillated between these alternatives, its actions depending largely on the availability of opportunities for expansion.[39] But whatever the disagreement, it did not seem to involve the question of expansionism as such. Oddly enough, the overthrow of the democracy in 411 and the ascent of the oligarchs, who did not share the democrats' enthusiasm for expansionism, did not bring a reversal of the imperialistic policy. One may in fact consider whether there was not substance in the persistent lamentations of Athenian envoys that there was no alternative to imperialism. Rather than rationalizing their actions, they were perhaps pointing to a very real and fundamental predicament. It is another curious phenomenon that—at least until the Sicilian débâcle—the extremists usually won out.

There may be good reason to explain the imperialistic policy in terms of the inherent traits of the democratic system under which the Athenians were living. Perhaps the uncertainties of a balance-of-power system without a balancer were a greater strain than the self-governing people could bear. The strong craving for a higher degree of security may well account for the adoption of aggressive policies which would provide emotional relief. Such anxieties as well as the desire for glory and economic gain doubtless were real factors in the politics of democratic Athens and could not but have an effect upon foreign policy. But they cannot be accepted as the entire explanation unless it can be shown that the imperialistic course was devoid of strategic rationality.

Since the imperialist transformation coincided with the adoption of an anti-Spartan policy, the most compelling explanation is strategic. The only reliable defense lay in preventing an upset of the precarious military equilibrium peculiar to the bipolar balance. It was imperative to deny the opponent a chance for military preponderance. What better assurance was there than the augmentation of one's own power? Political survival therefore clearly seemed to demand a tight security of one's possessions and, if possible, increased security through additional acquisitons. The rationale of bipolarism, then, explains to a large extent why there was no apparent alternative to imperialism and why allied secessions or other breaches of discipline were not met with greater tolerance.

Problems of empire

Instability of alliances—The transformation of a freely assumed contractual relationship based on mutual consent into imperial rule was to create international problems of its own. Contrary to what one might expect, the difficulty of exercising control was not thereby reduced to a simple administrative operation; relations between the leading powers and their allies became increasingly complex. No simple formula can express the intricacies of the imperial structures. These systems, if we may call them such, were not static; nor did they ever develop into a simple one-way relationship enabling the hegemonial power to make the allies do its bidding. What we find instead is a measure of fluidity, with allies changing sides and more or less successfully resisting their leader.

It may seem strange at first sight that this should have been so. One should be able to assume that the rigidity of the bipolar policy of the leading powers and their overwhelming strength had so reduced the independence of the smaller states as to make them pliable instruments in the hands of their masters. But the allies in fact could occasionally exercise some choice in affiliations. This latitude resulted from the contestants' active competition for supporters, which had played a role of some importance before the war and which became a major facet of policy after the outbreak of open hostilities. The fact that any defected state could confidently expect a warm welcome in the opposing alliance enabled smaller states to exploit the overtures made by the competitors for their own political advantage. The temptation to play the two giants against each other was too strong to resist. Although necessity often forced smaller states to take sides, they were alert to any sign of weakness on the part of the hegemonial power which would enable them to assert some measure of independence.

The scope of free choice further broadened after Sparta developed a first-rate navy, since equally effective protection could now be secured from either side. It is true of course that changes in alignment were not uncommon as a follow-up of domestic changes from democratic to oligarchic control and *vice versa*. An especially good example is Argos, which constantly wavered between Athens and Sparta depending on whether the democrats or the oligarchs were in control.[40] However, such considerations, as will be shown later on, were not as powerful as is often thought and lost in importance as the war became more intense.

A few examples of the allies' vacillations may suffice to show the nature of such fluctuations and the anxieties which they caused the leading powers. The Atheno-Spartan competition enabled Megara, probably in the early 450's, to leave the Peloponnesian Confederacy over a boundary dispute with Corinth and join the Delian League.[41] In 426 Athenian power was notably impaired by the decisions of the Acarnanians and Corcyreans to withdraw their active support and refuse further cooperation when Athenian aspirations became too ambitious.[42] The same year the Acarnanians and Amphilochians also refused to aid the Athenian attack on Ambracia for fear that Athens might become too powerful.[43] The wavering of allies was especially marked in the mass defections which followed the Athenian disaster in Sicily.

The high point of allied independence was reached with the conclusion of the Peace of Nicias. The fact that both leading powers were vying for their favor and the possibility that the breathing spell in the war might lead to a realignment permitted the small states to occupy briefly a prominent position in international politics. Argos, encouraged by Athenian support, now had reason to aspire to a hegemonial position in the Peloponnese. Sparta was understandably concerned. Irritated by the terms of the peace, many of the Peloponnesian states were aligning themselves with the hostile Argos, and eventually a pact challenging Sparta's hegemony was concluded between Athens, Argos, Mantinea, and Elis. It was the anxiety produced by this adverse political constellation and not a community of interests which induced Sparta to enter into the strange alliance with its erstwhile adversary. Not only did it expect thereby to diminish any trouble that might come from Argos, but apparently also to forestall additional threats from other Peloponnesian quarters.[44] If such were the initial expectations, the alliance proved of little help. When Sparta finally restored its hegemonial authority in the Peloponnese, it did so through unilateral military action, which ended in its victory over the anti-Spartan coalition at Mantinea in 418.

Under these circumstances the highly valued allied support could not always be secured through overt control. Friendly persuasion frequently proved a more effective method. Athens was less favorably situated in this respect than Sparta, partially because of Athens' harshness toward its allies in case of insubordination. The resentments which this had aroused were aggravated by the prevalence of democratic governments which Athens had helped establish in many allied cities. Not only were democratic governments more prone than other types to resist external control, but the Athenian prestige was likely to suffer doubly as a result of a seeming disregard of the much-praised democratic freedom. It is therefore little wonder that Athens should frequently have been compelled to resort to force in keeping its obstreperous allies in line.

Autonomist aspirations—In rallying around Athens, the members of the Delian League were not abjuring the rather extreme individualism characteristic of the Greek states whose highly developed sense of independence resisted subordination to another power. The Athenians found them less than tractable instruments for the realization of their own ambitions. This is not to say that particularism was so pronounced as to preclude effective cooperation within the context of a hegemonial system. But the autonomist sentiments severely limited the degree of conformity which the hegemonial power could expect to exact. To make things more difficult, the extent to which the allies would yield to the pressures of the leading power was not always easy to anticipate, inasmuch as the often-invoked "autonomy" did not have a clear and stable meaning. The practical minimum seems to have varied with time and place depending on political circumstances.

Normally, autonomy meant little more than "to have and use one's own laws," [45] that is, for all practical purposes freedom in the choice of constitutional form and independence in the conduct of internal affairs.[46] It did not commonly signify either freedom in the conduct of foreign affairs or the right to withdraw from a treaty of alliance.[47] But the term was elastic enough to be used in a variety of senses. At times it referred to complete independence, internal and external; at other times it meant no more than freedom from interference in internal affairs. In no case did it exclude the payment of a mutually agreed upon tribute.[48] It is debatable whether "autonomy" could be invoked to resist the collective decisions of an alliance; but unlike imperial rule (*arche*), membership in a hegemonial alliance alone did not imply the surrender of autonomy or submission to ultimate control.[49]

Hegemony then implied a rather precarious balance of self-determination in internal and subservience in external affairs. It was therefore more than likely that sooner or later hegemony would clash with autonomy.[50] According to a statement attributed by Thucydides to the Corinthians, "to take care of the common welfare" was the hegemons' duty "in return for the honors accorded them."[51] This requirement necessitated recurrent interferences with delinquent members' internal concerns. The difficulty of maintaining a reasonable balance of rights and obligations, therefore, was an exacting task even for the most enlightened *hegemon,* its success depending less on a sincere respect for the allies' independence than on tactical need.

In Thucydides' account the tone of the Athenians' relations with the allies was largely determined by expediency.[52] The difficulties that developed arose most frequently from financial reasons. The allies were bitterly resentful of the onerous tributes which Athens had imposed in order to meet the high cost of maintaining a navy and the demands of its citizens, who expected the democratic state to insure their material welfare. Obviously the autonomy of the allies was to suffer serious setbacks as a result of the numerous enforcement actions through which the Athenians held delinquents to their obligations. In the face of Athens' overwhelming power the allies were helpless. In fact, paradoxically, their strong individualism was ultimately responsible for the accelerated decline of their autonomy.

The allies soon awakened to the fact that the Athenians were amassing a far-flung empire, which neither verbal embellishments nor the high degree of autonomy Chios, Lesbos, and Samos were still enjoying could conceal. Before long Athenian rule came to be looked upon as even more odious than Persian domination.[53] The desire to remain autonomous meant more to them than the many material benefits of membership in the empire. Athenian support of democracy could only alienate the educated classes. As for the masses, they were not sufficiently deluded by the attainment of a desirable form of government to overlook the oppressive nature of their relationship with the Athenians.[54] If they nevertheless gave their support to the Athenian cause, they did so for fear of revenge and of the tyrannical rule of their own oligarchs.[55] But in most instances, their desire for autonomy stood higher in their scale of values than the love of democracy.[56]

In view of such tensions it cannot be assumed that the Athenians operated under the delusion that they could convert their alliance into a monolith. They apparently knew that tact and restraint were essential to maintaining the goodwill which the popular factions in most allied cities were showing them. It was a measure of their prudence that they retained the federate type of organization within the league. An alliance of formally independent and equal states, even if it was no more than a façade, certainly appeared more promising than overt imperial rule.[57] Hence the allies were allowed considerable latitude in self-government as long as they toed the line;[58] and if circumstances required a tightening of political control, concessions were frequently made in other areas. An illustration is the reduction of tributes in 450–49 to assuage the feelings aroused by interventions which were necessitated by the separatist efforts of local aristocrats.[59] Occasionally special concessions were made either because of enforcement difficulties or to reward loyal allies. The most meaningful was perhaps the granting of permission for allies to receive Pontic grain shipments directly, in exception to the normal practice of directing them by means of supervisory officers stationed at the Hellespont (*Hellespontophy-lakes*) to Piraeus from where they were distributed under Athenian supervision.[60]

There would seem to be reason to expect that Sparta was less plagued by the difficulties which autonomism posed. Although the allies were pledged to support Sparta's foreign policy and not to secede, the structure of power and early practice within the league reflected a degree of liberality that contrasted favorably with that prevailing within the Athenian system. However, in the long-run Sparta could not evade the problems created by the independence of the allies any more than could Athens; and when the allies—encouraged perhaps by the latitude allowed them—offered resistance, Sparta was sufficiently embarrassed, as has been seen, to apply controls not unlike those of the Athenians. True, instances are on record to show that Sparta's tolerance persisted even in cases of outright insubordination, as, for example, during the Peace of Nicias. But in this particular instance, its forbearance may possibly be attributed to considerations of political expedience. It is entirely conceivable that Sparta anticipated that the peace would be ephemeral and therefore was not at all displeased by its allies' continued hostility toward Athens. In general, Sparta's repeated resort to military measures against defectors shows clearly enough two things: first, the disturbing effect of autonomism within its league and, second, the seriousness with which the problem was viewed.

Bases of cohesion—In appraising the underlying reasons for resistance to hegemonial control, what stands out most clearly is the lack of common trust and mutual sympathy. Disunity prevailed, in spite of the traditional sense of a Greek cultural community in contradistinction to the Persians and other non-Greek peoples. The further attenuation of intra-Hellenic moral and social bonds can perhaps be attributed to the political polarization, which was rendering the maintenance of unity among a vast number of states with greatly diverging needs and interests a task of extraordinary difficulty. The high degree of military cooperation which can nevertheless be observed seems to have had an opportunistic basis, as is well illustrated by Thucydides' observation that in the battle of Syracuse in 413 alliances were determined by interest and compulsion.[61] In his view, then, the chief rationale for military cooperation lay in the *hegemon*'s ability and readiness to provide protection.

The Athenian success in making the formula work was due largely to the favorable image it had managed to create of itself in the early stages, still held in many quarters, of a protector who could provide substantial advantages to those who accepted its lead. The chief benefit to be derived from such an association consisted in an enormous extension of the area of peace through the coordination of a large number of states, which were no longer free to war against each other.[62] In addition, the common commitment and Athens' power afforded the members increased security against attacks emanating from without the circle of the league.[63] As for the overseas Greeks and the more exposed insulars, they could scarcely remain unimpressed by the Athenian success in emancipating outlying areas from Persian rule and reducing the Persian threat to the islands.[64] There was therefore a strong incentive to accept obligations toward the league and the protector, even if they frequently were burdensome.

Although interest was normally an adequate basis for a working relationship, it was not always reliable. For the leading powers in particular, associations so grounded involved two hazards. One was the possibility that protection would cease to be a central issue, either because political considerations might prevent them from providing it or because the need for protection might vanish with the reduction of the common enemy. In fact, both Sparta and Athens had to face up to separatist tendencies on the part of their allies as such contingencies arose. Just before the outbreak of the war Sparta was confronted by the Corinthians with the threat that they would secede from the Peloponnesian Confederacy because of Sparta's failure to protect their interests.[65] Similar tendencies developed after the conclusion of the Peace of Nicias when Sparta's failure to provide continued protection against Athenian imperialism caused a secessionist movement among its allies.[66]

Athens had similar experiences. When during a quarrel between Samos and Miletus in 441–40 Athens ordered Samos to cease hostilities and submit to Athenian arbitration, Samos revolted.[67] Perhaps the best example showing the effect of a diminishing need for protection is the lessening of the Persian threat. Considerable restiveness among the allies followed the Athenian victory over the Persians at the Eurymedon River about 467. Although a splendid demonstration of Athens' ability to provide the protection desired by Ionians and insulars, the seeming elimination of the Persian threat appeared to have removed the need for the hegemonial alliance. The further evaporation of the Persian threat with the conclusion of the Peace of Callias put an additional strain

on the discipline within the Athenian empire, as the apparent de-
crease of the number of tributary allies would suggest.[68]

The cohesion of alliances so grounded evidently depended largely
on the continued prestige of the hegemonial states, and this created
the second hazard. The allies' interpretations of their interest frequently varied with changing estimates of the belligerents' power
and gained in complexity with the varying fortunes of domestic
factions in their political struggle. Loss of prestige by the leader
often worked to attenuate the allegiance of wavering satellites who,
resentful of hegemonial domination, were quick to exploit any
show of weakness on the part of the leading state. But unfortunately for the allies, the sword in the hands of a protector could also
be turned against them. As the record shows, the protectors did
not hesitate to apply coercion, where other means failed, to keep
the imperialistic systems intact.

The Athenian and, to a lesser extent, the Spartan alliance
policies rested on the assumption that ultimately their empires
could be held together only through force. That view is hard to
refute. It is perhaps unnecessary to cite exhaustive proofs. A
few examples will suffice to illustrate the point. When in 441–40
Samos challenged Athenian authority, it was Athens' superior
military power which restored discipline.[69] The unwavering loyalty
of the Plataeans too had its basis in the fear of punishment that
Athens was able to inflict upon them.[70] By 427 Athens had become
widely unpopular with its allies, but, except for the defection of
Mytilene, its overwhelming power enabled it to hold the empire together. In the battle of Syracuse too it was power which kept the
allies on the Athenian side.[71] Although the loyalty of the continental allies was in some instances attributable to their hatred of
Sparta, the insulars certainly could ill afford to flout the mistress of
the sea.[72] Normally, military power could be used to good advantage
also to restore Athenian authority when it was challenged by allied
defections, and it effectively accomplished what good will and interest could not. A case in point is the effect of the impressive display of power at Sphacteria in 425, which enabled Athens to

double and treble tributes without encountering resistance and to levy payments even on states outside the empire.[73]

The Spartans also depended on military power for cementing alliances. Even their general Brasidas, reputed for his success in evoking admiration and sympathy for Sparta among the lesser states, was fully aware of the inadequacy of lofty arguments and pleasing generalities for securing loyalties. He, too, found intimidation and force useful and at times necessary aids.[74]

If there were obvious advantages in a timely and judicious display of power, an imprudent and immoderate show of strength, however, could do irreparable harm. One of the more obvious adverse effects would be the creation or consolidation of a hostile alliance. A good illustration is the peace made by warring Sicilian cities at the Congress at Gela in 424 out of fear of Athenian ambitions.[75] Another consequence might be the alienation of allies.[76] In effect, then, a show of strength, if discreetly employed, usually was an effective method for maintaining the power structure within an alliance system; but it was not a formula that could be applied universally and indiscriminately. The contrast between the Athenian and the Spartan practice is here instructive, inasmuch as Sparta's inclination to practice greater leniency often minimized the danger of disintegration.

The beneficial results of carefully considered and strategically timed leniency were appreciable, but they should not obscure the close relationship between the stability of the hegemonial systems and the fortunes of war of the hegemonial powers. The Athenians harbored no illusions as to the disastrous consequences that might result if they showed any great weakness. They had been faced with a crisis within the Delian League following their defeat in Egypt in 454. Mytilene defected as early as 428 since it believed Athens had been weakened by the plague, the death of Pericles, and the depletion of its finances.[77] In 426 the Ozolian Locrians went over to the Peloponnesians judging the Athenian cause lost.[78] Similar upsets followed the Athenian defeat at Amphipolis in 423 when many of the allies, encouraged by Brasidas' admonitions and generous promises, were either ready to or actually did defect. It was only upon the arrival of Athenian garrisons that they discovered that they had underestimated Athens' power.[79] Eventually, the defected Mende was reconquered[80] and Scione reduced.[81] The most severe blow was the Sicilian disaster, which resulted in the virtual disintegration of the Athenian empire. Although Athens managed to recoup some of its losses by recovering Chios,[82] Lebos,[83] Clazomenae,[84] and Lampsacus,[85] increased force was now required to hold the empire together.

It was no accident that separatism should have flourished particularly during the Peace of Nicias. The fact that neither of the superpowers now appeared as formidable as before encouraged third states to attempt forming an independent bloc. It is worth observing that the organization of an independent force was mostly at the expense of the Peloponnesian League. Evidently, Sparta's "betrayal" had outraged its allies and set off the spark of revolt. But it is unlikely that this alone would have produced a wave of defections had not Sparta's temporary weakness created the expectation that such self-assertion would be successful. It is also of interest to note that when Sparta eventually restored imperial discipline, it could do so only by resorting to force.

For a number of reasons the peace did not produce similar repercussions within the Athenian empire. Athens, unlike Sparta, had no moral position to maintain and was therefore free to make any settlement with the enemy that appeared expedient. Here Athens' relative indifference toward the moral problem turned out to be a source of strength. In addition, there were two institutional factors to account for the difference between the repercussions in the Spartan and the Athenian empires. Athens had dealt harshly with any attempt by an ally to rise to a leading position. Although this had produced considerable bitterness, it had also made the allies submissive as long as Athens seemed strong enough to hold them down. By contrast, Sparta's greater leniency could not but encourage expressions of self-assertion. The other reason lay in the very nature of a maritime empire. It was to Athens' distinct advantage that its dominion was over the insular world, whose territorial dispersion discouraged any attempts at collusion on a large scale. Sparta's alliance, on the other hand, extending over a compact territory, had no built-in safeguards against the pooling of resources that would provide the basis for an independence movement.

Imperialistic overextension—Considering the record, it seems strange that the Athenian empire should have come in for universal condemnation whereas the Spartan system has been more charitably described as one resting on consent rather than imperial rule. A number of explanations suggest themselves. Tradition had accustomed the Hellenic world to Sparta's leading position, which had been attained under less dramatic circumstances than those accompanying the rise of Athens. Moreover, Sparta was constrained by both national character and domestic institutions to practice moderation in the exercise of its power. But above all the need to coerce its allies was greatly reduced by the fear which Athens had managed to inspire everywhere and which enabled Sparta to seize the part of Panhellenic liberator. Under these conditions the consolidation of control over those who had voluntarily entrusted themselves to its protection involved little difficulty.

Athens was less fortunately situated. With the elimination of the Persian threat its alliance seemed to have lost its purpose. Yet maintaining maritime dominion required larger funds than could be raised at home by a faction-ridden democratic government. The simplest solution, therefore, seemed to be to shift the financial burden to allied cities.[86] In addition, the new Athenian empire suffered from uncertainties and resistances which confront all new rulers, whereas Sparta could confidently rely upon its universally acknowledged military superiority and the readiness of other oligarchies to defer to its wishes in return for support of their shaky political orders.[87] It would appear then that Sparta's seemingly enlightened rule was the result of favorable circumstances rather than of superior virtue. The record shows quite clearly that when conditions were less favorable, Sparta was not inhibited by a high regard for its allies' autonomy from adopting methods that were as ruthless as those for which Athens was generally censured. Although the alarm which Athenian imperialism evoked among contemporaries is understandable enough, it provides little grounds on the surface for the harsh censure to which Athenian practice was universally subjected in view of the similarity between its purposes and those pursued by Sparta. However, the main subject of controversy actually has not been so much expansionism *per se* as the extent of Athens' imperialist aspirations, and this does in fact raise disconcerting questions. To throw some light on the problem, it will be necessary to distinguish between reasons inherent in the political setting and the extension of power beyond limits that were politically and morally justifiable.

The first thing to be noted is that the Athenian practice was not wholly devoid of ideal conceptions in its earlier stages. Neither was the imperialistic development exclusively the responsibility of the Athenians, inasmuch as their city's rise to a dominant position presupposed the acquiescence and in some measure the active support of the allies.[88] Nor could it fairly be said that Athens' imperial rule was an unmitigated evil. It should in fact give us pause that even Aristotle seems to commend rather than censure the Athenians for acquiring a maritime empire.[89] Thucydides in turn leads us to believe that Pericles, the chief strategist of Athenian imperialism, envisaged Athens' role in the empire not only as that of a political but also of a spiritual leader providing an education for all Hellas.[90] Isocrates' eulogies on Athens' aspirations and practices,[91] though written after the Peloponnesian War, are helpful in explaining the psychology of what very likely was a sizable segment of the Athenian imperialists. What was condemned by others as the enslavement of Hellas appeared to them as enlightened rule. It was such optimistic views which apparently led Pericles to regard submission to Athenian rule as fair compensation for the physical protection provided and for the many advantages that followed from close ties with the great cultural center.[92] However, the edifice of noble sentiments eventually was to crumble. Lofty ideals were no safe barrier against a progressively brutal exercise of power. The enlightened leadership which Athens provided during

the early years of the Delian League vanished, and its domination
became increasingly oppressive in the sharpening struggle for hegemony.

Their failure to realize the noble vision of an empire based on a
solicitous paternalism and reciprocated by the allies' filial devotion
did not have a restraining effect upon the expansive ambitions of
the Athenians. Neither the expansionist tendencies inherent in
naval power nor strategic needs vis-à-vis Sparta created an atmosphere conducive to self-restraint. If a comprehensive consensus
among the allies was not obtainable, the prudent answer did not
appear to the Athenians to lie in the relaxation of control, since
this could easily be mistaken for weakness and therefore was likely
to encourage large-scale defections. But the substitution of force
for consensus as the bond of union set off an unfortunate chain
reaction. The resentments of the allies became increasingly bitter
as Athens applied coercion, and their growing resistance in turn
provoked progressively harsh measures on the part of the
Athenians.[93] The spectre of being isolated and perhaps becoming
the target of vengeful allies convinced the Athenians that under
no circumstances could they abandon the empire. In fact, fear as
the mainspring of an increasingly extreme and tenacious imperialism is a recurrent theme in Thucydides' account. Perhaps the most
striking expression of the compulsive basis of Athenian imperial
policy is the statement of the Athenian envoy Euphemus at
Camarina in Sicily during the great Sicilian campaign: "We are
rulers in order not to be subjects." [94]

The intensification of Athenian imperialism naturally gave rise to
ambitious plans for further conquests. The extension of power
produced growing appetites which were not easily contained. No
sooner had their sights reached the far corners of the Hellenic
world than the Athenians were casting greedy looks in new directions. Sicily was beckoning as a desirable object for conquest, and
before long the Athenians were envisioning an extension of their
dominion to Carthage and possibly the limits of the inhabited and
civilized world.[95]

The excesses of Athenian imperialism have customarily been

blamed on the extremism and moral deficiencies of the demagogic leaders who succeeded Pericles. Yet on careful reading of Thucydides' story, the responsibility does not appear as clear as is commonly assumed. Whether the demagogues were moved by unreasonable ambitions or whether they acted as they did because no other practical choices were available, their actions cannot be excused as a common human failing. It is true enough that strong and vigorous states normally seek to extend their control over alien peoples and that maritime powers in particular are prone to yield to the temptations of power. But such "natural" tendencies are no more acceptable than is unrepressed greed in individual men. The matter is different when it touches the bases of political existence. When states expand out of a justified fear for their security, moral censure ceases to be appropriate. No doubt it may often be difficult to say when fear is the actual spring of action and when it is a mere pretense invoked as a screen for ambition. Nevertheless the distinction must be made.

In the contest between Athens and Sparta it was less impulse or greed than mutual fear which underlay their respective imperialistic policies. Under the given conditions such a fear can hardly be dismissed as baseless. Since the feeling of insecurity, which the presence of an approximate military equilibrium had created, could be reduced only through self-reliance, the contestants understandably acted under a constant compulsion to acquire additional strength. Of course there were periods of apparent contentment. For example, no expansion of any consequence took place on either side at the height of the Periclean period between 449 and 435. But this extended tranquility was deceptive. As subsequent events were to show, it in no way signified the abandonment of expansionist ambitions; and as the bipolar struggle became more intense, we witness a resurgence of imperialistic activities rising to ever-greater heights during the war. Thucydides in fact does not permit us to forget the very real security dilemma which lay at the bottom of both Athenian and Spartan imperialism.

All this is not to say that greed and ambition played no part or that nothing the Athenians or the Spartans did in the name of security is beyond moral judgment. But even assuming that the leading powers were moved solely by a justified concern for their security, it would still have been inordinately difficult to define limited goals that could relieve their anxiety. Not surprisingly therefore, existing disagreements between different political factions were not cast in terms of imperialism versus anti-imperialism but referred only to secondary issues such as the scope of expansionist aspirations and the methods of imperial rule. A good illustration is the dispute among the Athenian factions over the treatment of the defected Mytilenians—with Cleon and Diodotus representing respectively the views of the extremists and the moderates. In counseling moderation Diodotus did not raise the fundamental issue of imperialism but took issue only with Cleon's extremism in demanding the death sentence for the defected city's people.[96]

An especially heated controversy ensued in Athens over the plan to attempt the conquest of Sicily, which was advocated by Alcibiades and opposed by Nicias. The fundamental political issues involved could be reduced to the two questions—neither of them easy to answer—whether it was possible to bring expansion to a halt and stabilize present possessions or whether the security of the empire could be insured only through ceaseless expansion. At first sight Nicias' cautiousness appears the sounder policy and in line with Pericles' counsel of moderation.[97] Alarmed by the passions which his war policy had released, the great statesman had earnestly pleaded for restraint at the outbreak of the war and warned his compatriots against new conquests that might involve them in unnecessary dangers.[98] By contrast, Alcibiades in effect questioned the applicability of Pericles' warning to the conditions that were now confronting Athens. His position that the empire could be secured only through continuous conquest and sustained aggressiveness[99] cannot be lightly dismissed, and it is at least questionable whether he was not actually the more accurate interpreter of Pericles' basic thoughts.

In assessing the compatibility of Alcibiades' plan with Pericles' policy, it must be remembered that Pericles had been chiefly responsible for raising the imperial edifice to its greatest heights and that he had done nothing to stop earlier brutalities and aggressions against the allies. In his last speech cited by Thucydides Pericles unequivocally expressed his opposition to any policy that would impair the security of the empire. While candidly admitting that the acquisition of the empire was of questionable morality, he was emphatic that it must be preserved to avoid disaster.[100] There is no need to interpret this exhortation as a reversal of his earlier position favoring restraint. His warning against excessive ambitions then had referred to risky and ill-conceived conquests undertaken for the sake of self-gratification without regard to strategic needs. His solicitude was clearly directed against willful assumption of *unnecessary* dangers unrelated to questions of security. But he nowhere implied that there were any alternatives to incurring risks when the empire was in danger.

The point in question then is whether the Sicilian expedition was strategically necessary to protect the empire and, if so, whether the risks involved were so great as to put the plan beyond the pale of rational calculation. Although it is never possible wholly to eliminate chance from military estimates, a good case can be made for the expedition. Thucydides did not consider it wrong in conception but attributed the disastrous outcome to the political disorder prevailing at home.[101] It is also doubtful that Pericles, had he been alive, would have rejected the plan as a willful assumption of unnecessary dangers. One may of course wonder whether the plan would have materialized without the intercession of personal forces, such as the agitation of the ambitious Alcibiades and the infatuation of his followers with the vision of a glorious future to be ushered in by the extension of Athenian rule over the entire Mediterranean. But personal ambition and collective dreams of glory are not what concerns us here. They are incidental to the problem under consideration; that is, what policy made most sense from the point of view of Athens' objective strategic needs.

Events between 446 and 431 had clearly revealed that it was impossible to stabilize the bipolar balance, and the persisting instability seemed to leave no other practical alternative than to step up competition in armaments, political influence, and expansion abroad. It appeared more than likely that the Sicilians—Dorian kinsmen of the Spartans and markedly inclining to the Peloponnesian side—would soon come to the aid of Athens' enemies. The consequences arising from such a dislocation of the balance of power would be sufficiently disastrous to justify preventing action even at great risk. On the positive side the conquest of Sicily had the advantage of strengthening Athens' military position by providing further naval strongholds, additional food supplies, and creating the requisite conditions for completing the blockade of the Peloponnesians. At the same time, it would relieve domestic economic pressure as the enthusiasm with which the lower classes supported the plan seems to suggest.[102]

The prospects of the expedition seemed favorable enough. It was uncertain and perhaps even unlikely that Sparta would muster enough initiative and daring to aid the distressed Sicilians, who were in desperate need of outside help.[103] Nor did it appear likely that the normally disunited Sicilians were capable of concerted action.[104] Yet the Athenian estimate erred, as Nicias correctly perceived,[105] in two essential respects. Their calculations seriously underestimated the determination of the Spartans, who realized quite clearly how closely their own security was linked to the Sicilians' ability to resist and how decisive the Sicilian campaign would be for the outcome of the war. If Sparta's apparent inertia, as Nicias had suspected, proved a trap, the risk of becoming irretrievably involved in a remote campaign was immense, especially since there was a good possibility that the war might be resumed at home. Perhaps neither Spartan succor to Sicily nor the war of attrition which Sparta began to launch from Decelea in Attica in 414 could have been foreseen, although these were possibilities which careful statesmanship could hardly afford to ignore. Still, Thucydides insists that the expedition would have succeeded had not the Athenians, for reasons of domestic politics consisting largely of petty jealousies, recalled Alcibiades before he could carry out his grand design. He in no way suggests that the plan was impractical or in any way incompatible with the strategic needs of the moment. Athenian blunders in the execution of the expedition were compounded when they continued their efforts in Sicily after the commencement of the Decelean War.[106] Even then the day might still have been saved by a strategic withdrawal of their forces.

Very likely, then, there would have been no basic disagreement between Pericles and his successors as to the permissible scope of Athens' imperialistic aspirations. Cleon's insistence that there was no room for sentimentalities when the existence of the empire was at stake[107] seems entirely in line with Pericles' own thinking; and his candid admission that the Athenian empire was a tyranny is merely a reverberation of words previously used by Pericles.[108] However, it is less likely that Pericles would have been a party to identifying reason of state with expediency pure and simple. It was one thing to suppress the defection of the Mytilenian allies; it was a matter of a different order to pronounce the death sentence on the people, as Cleon proposed to do. It may have appeared expedient enough to instil fear in rebellious subjects, even through brutal means,[109] in order to reinforce imperial control. But men's inclination to regard as justifiable what is advantageous and to excuse even the most monstrous atrocities in terms of strategic expediency is never a plausible defense. It seems unlikely that Pericles would have invoked reason of state or any other doctrine of state to justify the indefinite extension of utility in total disregard of the postulates of rudimentary humaneness.

Thucydides' own assessment of Athenian imperialism has been a moot point. As a result of his reticence to make his views on the subject explicit students have variously regarded him an anti-imperialist, an extreme imperialist, and a moderate imperialist. Attempts to classify his thinking in terms of such categories have not been generally successful. His implied and express criticisms of the Athenians and his undisguised antipathy for the post-Periclean architects of Athenian policy would make him appear at first sight an anti-imperialist. However, his acceptance of the Sicilian expedition as sound policy hardly seems reconcilable with such a position, nor does this put him in a class with the moderate imperialists.

His reticence either to praise or condemn may have resulted from the complexity of the political relations with which he was concerned and which did not permit simple judgments in terms of clear alternatives. He probably was neither for nor against imperialism in principle. He seems to have been quite willing to accept any policy that made sense in a given situation. It may well have been his opinion that under the existing conditions the Athenians had little choice but to expand as far as their power would permit. Perhaps it might still have been possible in the early days of the bipolar contest to practice a measure of restraint, when a wait-and-see policy would not preclude subsequent countermeasures if the opponent's ambition transgressed the bounds of what was tolerable. But after it became apparent that the mutual competition could not be halted and would become increasingly intense as time progressed, it would have been difficult to persuade either side to contain its expansive designs. The speeches of Cleon and Diodotus concerning the Mytilenian affair are here revealing. There is no reason to assume that they represent a departure from Thucydides' general method of presenting all sides of a problem and different views through antithetical speeches, leaving conclusions to the reader. Interestingly enough, neither speech questions the appropriateness of imperialism. This seems to support a presumption that not only the various Athenian factions but Thucydides himself saw no alternative.

Although Thucydides appears not to have regarded expansionism *per se* as the proper subject of censure, he leaves no doubt that he considered the Athenians wanting in circumspection and restraint. While there was at least a scrap of rationality in the expedition against Sicily, Athens' aspirations to conquer the Carthaginian empire and Etruria belonged in the realm of dreams. The same lack of judgment can be seen in the methods employed. The Sicilian venture was faulty in its execution, and the treatment of dependent or would-be dependent states repeatedly overstrained the tolerance of civilized men. But the transformation of the alliance system into an empire and the continuous striving of the contestants to round out their possessions was something for which neither the Athenians nor the Spartans could fairly be criticized and were not so criticized by Thucydides.

Thucydides' repeated references to the tyrannical rule which Athens exercised over its allies and to the allies' "enslavement" must be seen in this light. It is quite possible that he was referring to "enslavement" in the descriptive sense. The term is ambiguous but very probably, in this context, meant only that a state was in political subjection to another state.[110] In this sense it designates the *de facto* distribution of power in the relations of two states and is not, in and of itself, a term of opprobrium. The term "tyranny" has the more definitely moral connotation of oppressive rule. In so describing the Athenian empire Thucydides no doubt was conveying the feelings harbored by most contemporaries toward the Athenians. But to the extent to which such references reflect his own thinking, they can refer only to the manner in which power was exercised, not to the fact of domination.

NEUTRALS

The sharp alignment of powers not only reduced allies to the status of satellites but posed an actual and serious threat to the independence of neutral states as well. An examination of the record shows quite clearly that the gulf between neutral and aligned states was much narrower than might be supposed. This is not to say that the precarious status of neutrals was peculiar to the bipolar system. In fact their security in most major wars, embracing entire balance-of-power systems, has depended largely on the willingness of belligerents to respect neutrality. But what was characteristic of the bipolar struggle was the practical absurdity of neutrality from the moral as well as from the political point of view. A brief review of the fate of neutrals before and during the Peloponnesian War will illustrate the point.

As soon as the bipolar pattern began to emerge shortly after the Persian War, indications of a growing disregard of the leading powers for the preferences of third states can be observed. Perhaps one of the earliest expressions of anti-neutralism was Themistocles' advocacy of universal membership in the Panhellenic alliance.[111] With the Athenian conquests which followed, it became increasingly clear that whatever respect was shown for neutral rights was more a matter of convenience than the recognition of a legally defined status. If neutrality aroused misgivings in the leading powers while the storm clouds were gathering, it became anathema with the outbreak of the war. Before the war neutrality may have been frowned upon by the superpowers, but it was an honorable status in the eyes of the world at large. This ceased to be true with the outbreak of hostilities. The pressure to take sides, be it out of friendship or prudence, mounted steadily. There was much cogency in the warning of the Corinthians, on the eve of the war, against the neutralist self-deception of the inland states vis-à-vis the sustained economic and military pressures of Athenian imperialism.[112]

When the war broke out, Thucydides saw in it the greatest upheaval in the history of mankind and anticipated that before it was over all the Greeks would have taken sides.[113] His expectation was not far wrong. One power after another, barbarian as well as Greek, was pressured into participation. By 429 the Achaeans had joined the Peloponnesian League. In 426 Athens tried to enter into alliance with as many neutrals as possible, extending feelers—unsuccessfully, to be sure—to Sicily, Epirus, the Thracian king Sitalces, Thessaly, Argos, and even the Persian king.[114] Again, in 410 Athens tried to induce its former allies on the Ionian Sea to give up the neutrality which they had observed since the Sicilian disaster.[115] The most dramatic illustration of the plight of the neutrals was the case of Melos, which was repeatedly pressured by Athens to join its alliance system and, when it refused, was forcibly reduced.[116]

Although third states showed little impartiality toward the contest, most of the Greeks being sympathetic to the Spartan cause,[117] the only ones enjoying some measure of security in their neutral status were those strong enough to defend it by force of arms. A notable example were the West Greeks in Sicily, who, instead of living up to their commitments to the Peloponnesians, observed a benevolent neutrality which their geographic remoteness and great power permitted them to do.[118]

General intolerance of neutrality did not mean that the superpowers did not make occasional attempts to neutralize a lesser state. However, any such moves must be explained in terms of temporary expediency rather than a genuine readiness to accept neutralism. When Athens tried to neutralize Corinth in 419,[119] it evidently did so in the knowledge that there was not even a remote chance of bringing it over as an ally. The greatest possible advantage that could be gained was to detach it from Sparta.

In view of Sparta's apparent tolerance of neutrals, Archidamus' offer of neutrality to the Plataeans, allies of the Athenians, in the third year of the war is of considerable interest.[120] Actually, the offer was devoid of any practical meaning. Archidamus was fully aware that the Plataeans could not possibly defend themselves against such powerful neighbors as Athens or Thebes [121] and quite sensibly supplemented his offer with the suggestion that they turn their city over to Sparta for the duration of the war. These supplementary terms, aside from being a more or less transparent ruse of the Spartan king to transfer Plataea from Athenian to Spartan control, are notable also as an expression of his skepticism that an unprotected state of the size and capabilities of Plataea would be permitted to enjoy the blessings of neutrality in the midst of the great upheaval. The same skepticism appears to have been at the basis of Sparta's attitude toward Lesbos, which it admitted to its alliance after the island's defection from Athens in 428 in spite of inconvenient timing and the awkwardness of acquiring an insular ally.[122] Evidently, neutrality was not considered practicable under the political conditions of the moment.

Aside from such inferences as may be drawn from the events related, Thucydides' account contains a number of direct references to the incongruity of neutrality under the given conditions. The Corinthians for example warned the Spartans not to drive their allies into some other alliance.[123] Much in the same vein, the Athenians feared that all their defected allies would join the Spartans.[124] And the Spartan ephor Sthenelaidas exhorted his countrymen not to give up their allies to the Athenians.[125] Evidently in none of these cases was neutrality regarded a practicable alternative.

It is of course not surprising that with the bipolarization of power neutrality should have ceased to be a status that the belligerents would respect. Genuine neutrality, resting on independent strength rather than on the indulgence of the belligerents, presupposes the existence of a multiplicity of political units of roughly equal power. In a bipolar world, the great disparity of power between superpowers and others causes neutrality to depend entirely on the convenience of the superpowers, and situations where neutrality is equally advantageous to both sides are likely to be rare. A good indication of the misgivings of the leading powers concerning the feasibility of neutral status was the provision of the settlement of 446 which specifically designated uncommitted states as objects of competition between them.[126] Their mutual recognition of each other's hegemony in a reserved sphere, while acknowledging reciprocal freedom of action in regard to neutrals, was probably based on the expectation that sooner or later most states would be absorbed by the two great alliance systems. Usually there were good strategic reasons—apart from other, less tangible considerations that may have been influential—to commend the incorporation of neutrals. The case of Melos, the chief symbol of the plight of neutrals, furnishes a particularly good illustration. On the positive side, possession of the island would enable the Athenians to block the access of the Peloponnesians to Egypt.[127] On the negative side, the Athenians had reason to fear that the continued independence of a likely candidate for its alliance would be interpreted as a sign of weakness.[128] But aside from any specific reasons, the leading states could not have looked with general favor upon the neutrality of states that were unable to resist absorption by the opponent.

Considerations of practical convenience were soon to give rise to moral judgments cloaking anti-neutralism with legitimacy.[129] If neutrality was no longer a respected status, it also ceased to be a respectable status. It was not long before the contest took on aspects of a struggle between good and evil, in which neutrality was the object of moral reproof. It is not difficult to account for this tendency to think along moralistic lines. The division of Hellas had gone beyond the external relations of states, invading the realm of domestic affairs and producing a corresponding political and social schism.[130] The internal class struggle between the masses and the oligarchs had understandably created the belief that there was an analogous universal issue to be settled on the international plane.[131] As factional hatred gained in intensity neutrality was progressively tainted with the stigma of immorality.[132] Brasidas' lecture to the Acanthians instructing them in their duty to aid the side of freedom is a case in point.[133] The same sentiment was expressed in his high praise, resting on similar grounds, of Scione for having defected from Athens.[134]

To a large extent the war had assumed the character of internecine strife; factional division made the issues appear in terms of moral absolutes. The resulting penchant to classify all humanity in friend-enemy categories stamped the neutral as the enemy of both sides,[135] to be held in even greataer contempt (because of his moral indifference) than the forces of evil themselves. Sparta as the self-appointed defender of Hellenic independence particularly inclined toward the moralistic view. But the Athenians, though less given to moralizing, were equally disinclined to accept neutrality and rather contemptuously dismissed the sustained aloofness of the Corcyreans as a neutralist folly.[136] Evidently, then, both sides rejected, for ideal as well as for practical reasons, any status other than that of friends or enemies, subsuming the most diverse relationships under these all too simple and entirely subjective categories.

From the perspective of the small states too neutrality must have appeared anything but attractive. And even where neutral status implied advantages, considerations of security made participation appear preferable. Reasons of security were invoked by the Plataeans in rejecting Sparta's plea that they adopt a neutral position.[137] The need of the lesser states for big power protection was also emphasized by Brasidas when he was trying to convince the Acanthians that neutrality was impracticable.[138] Similarly, Hermocrates warned his Sicilian countrymen at Camarina against the dangers of neutralism.[139] But quite apart from such practical aspects, third states occasionally seem to have been afflicted with a sense of guilt over their nonparticipation. It is of interest to note that even the proud and independent island of Corcyra, a leading maritime power, should not only have admitted its imprudence in leaving itself exposed in the event of conflict with a major power but virtually to have apologized to the Athenians for its sustained neutrality.[140]

Further incentives for participation were provided by domestic politics.[141] Oligarchies in particular tended to rely heavily upon Sparta for protection against internal disturbances of a democratic nature and against conquest by the Athenians, which would signal the end of their political rule. But democracies had no less reason to avoid neutrality, since conquest by the Peloponnesians would mean the abolition of their constitutional orders. It is therefore hard to escape the impression that neutrality was anything but a promising status. This did not, to be sure, prevent defections from occurring with increasing frequency as the war progressed. However, such defections did not produce growing numbers of neutrals; rather, the need for protection led defected allies to seek membership in the opposing alliance system.[142]

Our contention that neutrality was generally unattractive to the lesser states at first sight seems refuted by the coordinated attempts made by Sparta's allies to create a third force in reaction to the Peace of Nicias, when the moment appeared auspicious. In actuality, however, the many defections of Peloponnesians were far from being inspired by neutralist sentiments. Sparta's allies were much too deeply involved in the fight against Athens to dream of such a luxury.[143] On the contrary, it would be more accurate to say that their anti-Athenian sentiments were stronger even than Sparta's and that it was Sparta's slackening leadership in the war that was responsible for such attempts to carry on the fight alone. Corinth's efforts in behalf of the independent league led by Argos served no other purpose than to steer Sparta back on the anti-Athenian course.[144] Once it had succeeded in this, Corinth gave up its independent efforts and rejoined Sparta's confederacy.[145]

chapter 5

THE ISSUES

The causes of any major war are complex and the issues manifold. The difficulty of ascertaining them is not lessened by the moral principles that are frequently invoked to surround international attacks, whether provoked or unprovoked, with an aura of legitimacy. The war between Athens and Sparta was no exception. What rendered the clarification of issues especially difficult was the seriousness with which recourse was made to principles and the readiness with which such claims were universally accepted. It seemed that here they were more than a transparent pretense. It will therefore be necessary to explore at some length the ultimate motivation of the contestants if the nature of the bipolar struggle is to be illuminated. Was it the purpose of Athens and Sparta to realize principles and ideals or to nail down their political supremacy? The answer is far from obvious.

At first sight the picture seems simple enough. The entire Hellenic world appears divided between two factions, the many (the *demos*) and the few (the oligarchs or aristocrats), each attempting to impose upon society its particular social and political organization. In this universal struggle for a way of life Sparta had taken up the cudgels for the oligarchs while Athens was identifying itself with the cause of the *demos*. Although it is easy to see why the cleavages caused by the bitter factional strife between the privileged and underpriviledged classes should have led many students to explain the political dualism in terms of conflicting ways of life, the record does not bear out such a simple causality. This is not to belittle the role which the clash of principles was to play in the war. Thucydides' vivid description of the factional strife shows clearly enough that few states involved in the conflagration were spared from inundation by the revolutionary wave.[1] Numerous episodes, surely, could be cited to support an analysis in terms of a contest between "good" principles and "bad" principles. Perhaps the quasi-religious overtones of the war are most dramatically highlighted by the exceptionally cruel vengeance the Athenians inflicted upon the recalcitrant Melians, which went far beyond the bounds of ordinary vindictiveness.

The presence of such elements, even if they had far-reaching effects, does not, however, prove that they were decisive. They gave no immediate clue to the order of priority which principle and interest were assuming in the thinking of responsible statesmen. Rather, the relevant test is whether statesmen were concerned with their city's security as a political unit or with winning a victory for a moral and political cause. The question merits special attention in the bipolar context, where the bifurcation of power had produced clearly drawn battle lines. The apparent simplicity of a contest in which almost everybody was aligned with the one or the other side easily suggested a similar simplicity of the issues involved. And if politics were viewed in terms of clear-cut issues, it is not surprising that the belief should have gained ground that the conflict was essentially moral in nature and that the moral issues which were its subject were equally clear and simple. With this assumption in mind it was easy to regard the military struggle for power as secondary to the fundamental clash between two contradictory ways of life, two antagonistic political orders, and ultimately between contradictory moral forces.

The fact that all of Greece viewed the contest largely as a fight for a way of life does not necessarily mean that it was similarly regarded by Athens and Sparta. They chimed in with the general moralizing, to be sure; but was this a definite indication of the objectives for which they were ultimately contending? Were they moved by the conviction that the antagonistic forces they represented could not possibly coexist within the area they considered their home and that they were therefore inescapably headed for a military showdown? For all the moral fervor pervading the political debate, the events leading up to the war unmistakably point to the primacy of power issues. It is above all extremely doubtful that a mutual adaptation of the Spartan and Athenian ways of life or a reconciliation of the hostile classes would have appreciably alleviated political tensions and the prevalent sense of military insecurity which were largely responsible for the outbreak of the war. Nor does the absence of a clear political pattern in the alignment of powers before the war seem to support the thesis that the course of events was determined by moral issues or even by class interests. A brief survey of the ultimate aspirations of the leading powers and their visions of the postwar world may serve to cast light upon the matter.

An earlier chapter called attention to the limited scope and the pragmatic nature of the goals of both belligerent parties at the outset of the war. What essentially was at stake was the protection of their political independence and the security of their possessions. From the Spartan point of view security required that the further growth of Athenian power be arrested, and this was what Sparta hoped to accomplish by making war after peaceable means had proved ineffective. There is no evidence to show that it set out to wage a war of annihilation. Its sustained hope of arranging terms, which persisted as late as 427,[2] suggests the moderateness of its goals. It seems unlikely that Spartan thinking would have been directed toward a settlement had the intention been to conduct a moral crusade. It may of course be objected that the Spartan ultimatum, requesting the Athenians to relinquish their empire, had all the necessary ingredients of a crusade. But the sweeping nature of the ultimatum very likely was the outgrowth of practical experience. The failure of recent attempts to contain Athenian power short of war seemed to admit of no other practical alternative than radical diminution or possibly even destruction of the empire. There is therefore no compelling reason to suspect Sparta of any but practical political motivations.

The issue nevertheless seems clouded by Sparta's strong moral indignation at Athenian transgressions and the apparent seriousness with which it seized the role of guarantor of Hellenic freedom against the threat of Athenian imperialism. But when all the facts are considered, Sparta's moral protestations, though gaining in frequency and vehemence as the war progressed, appear largely as a screen for the practical political interests it was trying to protect. Surely, had the Spartans been sincere about their alleged moral crusade, they would have been hard put to accept Alcibiades —ex-leader of the Athenian democratic faction and incarnation of the evil—as a consultant when he offered his services after falling into disfavor at home. It also gives pause that in 411 when the Athenian democracy was overthrown by the oligarchic faction, Sparta summarily rejected the latter's peace overtures.[3] True, the Athenian oligarchs were holding out for terms;[4] as Athenians they evidently were not willing to surrender their city uncondi- tionally. Nor did the overthrow of the democracy mean that the democratic forces could thereafter be ignored altogether. But even after everything else had failed, when they were ready to make peace at any price,[5] the war continued. What is decisive for the present argument is that here the bipolar conflict was not re- solved by the existence of oligarchic orders in the two battling states. Very probably Sparta's king Agis realized that a conflict of such seriousness and proportions as this could not be resolved short of the total defeat of the enemy city, regardless of who controlled its government.

Other examples of Sparta's pragmatism can be cited. Of interest are the arguments used by the Spartan general Brasidas in reas- suring the Acanthians in the midst of the war that his city's aim was not to erect an empire but to put one down. Moreover, his attempt at persuading them to join his side was not based on moral preachments but on power realities.[6] Perhaps an even clearer ex- ample is Sparta's offer of a joint hegemony with Athens after suffering a serious setback at Pylos.[7] Such an arrangement would certainly have been risky since the dynamic Athenians might well have succeeded in claiming a dominant position in the partnership. It is true that Sparta at that point might have been distressed by its unfavorable military position; but its situation was not so desperate as to offer an adequate explanation for taking so great a chance. Very likely Sparta was moved by a genuine desire to come to terms. A further example is the Peace of Nicias. Sparta's readiness to conclude the peace in the face of such obvious disadvantages as the surrender of its moral position and the alienation of its allies must be taken as fairly reliable evidence of a strong desire for a settlement. Perhaps the best example of Sparta's pragmatism is the conclusion in 412 of three treaties with the Persians. The surrender of the Greek brethren in Ionia to Persian rule and possibly Persian colonization did not seem too high a price for the opportunity to break the bipolar stalemate.[8]

All this does not necessarily suggest that Sparta was acting in a cynical spirit. The high stakes involved in the contest seemed to justify resort to any means within reason, and the claim to liberate Greece from the Athenian threat was too useful a means of propaganda to be ignored, providing as it did the needed focus for the anti-Athenian alliance. It is also not difficult to understand why the liberation sham should have fallen on fertile soil. When Greece was threatened by the Persian invasion, the Greeks had looked to Sparta for protection against Asian despotism. Now its reputation as liberator from tyranny was inspiring Hellenic solidarity under Sparta's aegis in the struggle against Athenian attempts at domination.[9] The Greeks were thus psychologically prepared to accept Sparta's protection and to take its professed altruism on trust.

Fortunately for Sparta, its interest in preserving the status quo blended admirably with the protection of Hellenic particularism against Athenian attempts to unite the Greeks under Athens' hegemony.[10] It was only with the Peace of Nicias that Sparta's image became tarnished and its promises of liberation were unmasked as empty propaganda slogans. Until that time, however, the liberation propaganda fully served its strategy of inducing

Athens' allies to defect. It was the liberation issue that enabled the Spartan general Brasidas to obtain the adherence of Acanthus, Amphipolis, Torone, Scione, and Mende;[11] and the same tack accounts for the success of the Spartan general Gylippus in stirring up the fighting spirit of his allies before the battle of Syracuse.[12]

The Athenian goals initially appear more extravagant. Pericles had rather sweepingly claimed that the Athenian dominion already extended not only to the allies but to the entire maritime sphere.[13] Alcibiades, the draftsman of later Athenian foreign policy, took an even broader view and candidly admitted his city's aspiration to worldwide rule.[14] However, such claims create a deceptive image of the Athenian statesmen's cast of mind. The difficulty of containing bipolar imperialism within definable limits was discussed in the preceding chapter. It must of course be admitted that here as in other respects Alcibiades is suspect of having been motivated by personal ambition, which was not easily curbed.[15] But the fact remains that neither he nor Pericles seriously attempted to justify or embellish their universalist aspirations through a resort to lofty principles. There certainly was nothing extravagant in Alcibiades' defense of the self-perpetuating tendencies of Athenian imperialism as an insurance "lest we be ruled by others." [16]

At first sight there may be understandable doubt that such an explanation can be accepted at face value. It would seem plausible enough to regard it as a mere device to elicit the support of his countrymen. Yet it is impossible to ignore the seriousness of the problem at hand; the compulsive effect which fear of the enemy's vengeance and of the imperial subjects' reaction should control be relaxed had upon Athenian thinking cannot be dismissed as without foundation. In these circumstances *ad hominem* arguments would seem insufficient grounds for rejecting the authenticity of Alcibiades' stated position.

Although with the passage of time the precedence of interest over principle became more obvious, moral principles continued to be invoked and, in spite of their opportunistic character, did not remain without effect upon the conduct of the war. The singular ferocity with which the war was fought is traceable to them. The fact that principles had only a tenuous relationship to the motivations of the leading powers did not prevent them from having a formidable impact upon the lesser states, who had no difficulty in equating morality with the needs of practical strategy and in accepting principles as guides for practical policy. This was the main basis of the enormous practical importance of principles in the contest. Once the peoples of Greece had become captives of the ideals proclaimed in their behalf, it was inevitable that an inordinately high premium should have been placed on propaganda as a means of warfare, regardless of the ends sought by the superpowers.

CONSTITUTIONAL CONFORMITY

The extent to which the ends sought by the belligerent parties were political in character, then, was not always wholly evident. The discrepancy between the real issue and the alleged aim of securing a given way of life and mode of political management was bound to generate considerable confusion. The nature of the contest was further obscured by the frequent efforts of the leading states to conform their actions to such professed goals. Time and again the observer is struck by their zeal in trying to remake the Greek world in their respective images by assimilating satellite and conquered cities into their own constitutional type. The strategic rationale of such endeavors is not immediately apparent. Frequently the disadvantages of such adaptations stand out more prominently than the advantages.

In Sparta's case constitutional assimilation can perhaps be reconciled easily enough with political interests. It was advantageous to deal with oligarchies since all that was required to control them was to control the oligarchs. Normally their foreign policies were unaffected by the erratic changes of mind of the *demos*. By contrast, democracies were less susceptible to hegemonial direction because of the central role played by a changing public opinion and the self-assertive tendencies that are characteristic of democratic governments.[17] This is not to say that democracies did not offer some rather appreciable advantages to the hegemonial state. Not only were they frequently more stable than oligarchies,[18] but a discontented *demos* was also highly receptive to propaganda and might therefore provide a lever for overcoming the resistance of obstreperous leaders.

It would therefore seem that under ordinary conditions a case could be made for Athens' policy of constitutional assimilation. Yet under the conditions which then prevailed the undeniable advantages were offset by serious drawbacks. At a time of social upheaval, democracies were especially receptive to propaganda of the nihilistic type and provoked considerable turbulence. The susceptibility of allied or dependent states to revolutionary outbursts alone was a heavy liability to the hegemonial power. But the usefulness of democratic governments was further diminished, as the Old Oligarch charges in his treatise on the Athenian Constitution,[19] by their proverbial undependability. Even if the well-known prejudices of that unidentified writer cast considerable doubt on the validity of his generalizations, this particular assertion seems psychologically plausible in view of the ease with which democratic assemblies could and normally would reverse themselves.

If strategic considerations do not provide an immediately satisfactory answer to the problem of constitutional conformity, it may be well, before pursuing this line of inquiry further, to look for an explanation in the realms of history or sociology. The assumption that a special affinity existed between states having identical or similar constitutional systems was generally accepted in the Greek world. That belief had its basis in historical experience. Sparta, in forming the Peloponnesian League, had used constitutional conformity as a weapon to protect oligarchic governments against the rising bourgeoisie and to secure and extend the league.[20] The matter became more serious with the reforms of Cleisthenes in Athens in 508 B.C., which marked the beginning of the Atheno-Spartan rift. The respectability which democracy was now acquiring by virtue of its success in the second powerful city could not but heighten the democratic challenge and give rise to the general feeling that oligarchic states would support each other just as a special bond seemed to unite democratic states.

There is much to be said for this assumption from the sociological point of view. Similarity of political form would normally provide a good foundation for a harmony of interests among allies. Between *hegemon* and followers it constituted a bond that was more solid and very likely more enduring than a temporary coincidence of interest or resort to force. There is no need to belabor the point that any lasting union requires inner cohesion and that this in turn presupposes a measure of homogeneity among its members.

However much merit there may be in these points, they do not provide adequate explanations in view of the highly political character of the contest. The supreme ends sought, as has been seen, were political, and the struggle for supremacy reduced all other aspirations to incidental importance. And from the political vantage point, democracies tended to be erratic and unreliable. Nor was this the time for sentimentality or for a crusade to make the Hellenic world safe for either democracy or aristocracy. Not even ethnic kinship and the long-standing tensions between Dorians and Ionians had any appreciable effect upon war strategy. If such things were referred to at all, it was largely for reasons of propaganda, and it was only in the sphere of propaganda strategy that they had any tangible importance. The relative insignificance of ethnic kinship comes out clearly in Thucydides' account. True, in appealing to the Sicilians to stand together in warding off the imminent Athenian attack, the Syracusan leader Hermocrates repeatedly invokes their common Dorian descent as well as the traditional enmity between Dorians and Ionians. But his speech stresses that the actual alignments in the great conflagration were not following ethnic lines, and he himself lays a heavier accent on the need to present a united front against the Athenian aggressors than to shield Dorians against Ionian intruders.[21] The idea stands out even more clearly in the reply of the Athenian envoy Euphemus to the effect that kinship was determined by political loyalty.[22]

Noting all this, it will be well to revert to the realm of political strategy for an explanation. Perhaps the best means of clearing the matter up will be first to examine the consistency with which Athens and Sparta pursued constitutional conformity and second to see whether, where they did so, political reasons can be found.

In the case of Sparta a few instances immediately come to mind where the presumed policy was abandoned. Although constitutional conformity was often insisted on, neither compassion nor constitutional similarity moved Sparta to come to the aid of the desperate Melians when they were confronted by the Athenians with the choice between submission and annihilation. Another departure from the alleged principle, which has already been alluded to, is the rejection of peace-feelers extended by the Athenian oligarchs after the overthrow of democracy in 411. A similar pragmatism can be detected in the politics of Brasidas who reassured the Acanthians: "I am not come to change your constitution," [23] and who after the capture of Torone spared no effort to win the friendship of the pro-Athenian faction.[24] He followed the same policy at Scione.[25]

Athens traditionally had shown little concern with the problem. As long as the allies performed their obligations, it had remained indifferent to their internal political arrangements.[26] However, with the passage of time the constitutional issue acquired more central importance. In the mid-460's the Athenians would still extend requested aid to the Spartans in their campaign against the rebellious Messenians and *helots,* though the democratic faction seems to have opposed it.[27] But with the final victory of the democracy in 462–61, which very likely was accelerated by Sparta's dismissal of the force the Athenians had dispatched, a greater emphasis was laid on the establishment of democratic governments elsewhere, either to subvert enemy states or to draw doubtful or defected allies closer to Athens.[28] Aid given to the popular factions in Thessaly and Boeotia in 457–56 [29] and interference in the internal affairs of Samos in 442 [30] are cases in point.[31] Yet on the whole the record is not sufficiently consistent to show that the Athenians felt compelled or committed to democratize the Hellenic world. Conforming allies were normally permitted to choose their form of government and even to retain oligarchic governments if such was their preference. What is more, Athens would not hesitate on occasion to support oligarchies and monarchies even against democratic forces if this seemed politically or strategically expedient.[32] Nor did the Athenians appear to have had any great qualms about attacking cities in Sicily having governments that were either identical or similar to their own type..

These fluctuations seem to suggest that the decisive criterion was strategic. Consequently, a closer look at the possible political value of constitutional conformity in the context of the Peloponnesian War will be in order. It will be recalled that the bipolarization of power was not only a phenomenon of international life but had also left its imprint on the structure of domestic politics. Everywhere cities were widely split between the contending factions, and in the bitterness of the strife, partisan interests tended to supersede those of the more comprehensive unit of the *polis*. In this struggle, which was simultaneously fought on the international and on the domestic plane, the democratic as well as the oligarchic factions would look for support wherever it was obtainable. What was more natural than that they should have adopted the two great states, one of whom symbolized the democratic and the other the oligarchic type, as their respective protectors?

The bitterness generated by the deep social cleavages throughout the Greek world after the victory of the populist forces in Athens and the gravity of the threat which democratic Athens seemed to represent to the oligarchic concept of civilization made the rival city appear to conservative eyes the necessary target of an oligarchic crusade. It was therefore only natural that in their predicament the oligarchs everywhere should have turned to Sparta for support, even if this meant surrendering their city's external independence.

It is no less understandable that Athens should have similarly enjoyed the sympathies of the *demos*. Quite obviously, the popular

forces were as fearful of the oligarchs as the oligarchs were of
them; and from the anti-oligarchic bias of the lower classes, there
arose a sense of community between the *demos* in the various
cities and the great power that symbolized its aspirations.[33] But
this feeling of solidarity in facing a common enemy and a craving
for protection were not the only bases of the pro-Athenian sentiment. Aside from such practical and opportunistic reasons, the
Athenian order seemed to be able to inspire a deeply felt positive
affection. Its most notable achievement responsible for evoking
such sentiments was the establishment of an admirable degree of
justice for all its citizens through legal equality (*isonomia*) at a
time when the old aristocratic orders (*eunomiai*) were deteriorat-
ing everywhere. What is more, legal equality became an increasingly
attractive idea when it was extended into the political realm
as an equal sharing by all citizens in the exercise of political
power.[34] Such a system seemed to form a refreshing contrast with
the political corruption which had become prevalent in most
oligarchies. An additional attraction was that a political order so
grounded promised to be extraordinarily stable, since the equal
distribution of political power in turn was likely to buttress obedi-
ence to the law.[35]

The ascendancy everywhere of party interests above the general
interests of the *polis*, then, goes far to explain the seeming mystery
of constitutional conformity. The deepening of internal cleavages
encouraged domestic factions to look for outside support and to
seek alliances across territorial lines. In this way Sparta and Athens
were to become factors in the domestic affairs of the lesser states,
and both were quick to grasp the strategic opportunities which the
factional alignment offered.[36] The scare induced by the spread
of democracies virtually forced Sparta to seize the championship
of the oligarchic cause; likewise, Athens could not remain indifferent to the strategic advantages that could be derived from the
sympathy which its constitutional form was enjoying among the
lower classes. It had reason to expect that a popular government
would insure a city's allegiance or accession to the Athenian alliance
system. Conversely, the displacement of popular control by the

oligarchic faction was likely to spell the end of Athenian influence. In fact, the guiding hand of the oligarchs could usually be detected in revolts against the Athenian hegemony,[37] and the Old Oligarch does not seem to have been far wrong in stating that the Athenians never had much luck in securing the support of the "worthiest" elements (*hoi beltistoi*).[38] The argument seems corroborated by Athenian experiences in relation to the Boeotian oligarchs, Miletus, Samos, and Mende.

Constitutional conformity was useful not only to insure the loyalty of one's allies, but also as a means of undermining the opponent's authority within his own camp. The spread of democratic movements especially proved an effective fifth column for the Athenians. As has been shown in an earlier chapter, the enormous mass appeal of democratic institutions alone caused Sparta to regard the very existence of the Athenian empire a threat to the security of its hegemonial system, particularly during the early phase of the war. But Sparta's apprehensions of the effect of democracy can be detected as early as the late 460's in its dismissal of the Athenian forces at Ithome for fear that their presence might have a revolutionary effect upon the besieged.[39] Although Sparta seems to have been slower in adopting fifth column methods, it eventually turned the Athenian weapon against Athens itself in stirring up revolts throughout the empire.[40] It was not too difficult to raise the spectre of a loss of independence as the result of too close an attachment to Athens.

In spite of such tendencies, constitutional conformity was not an unvarying success in actual practice. On the positive side, considerable evidence can be marshalled to show the appreciable strategic advantages of political homogeneity and the liabilities resulting from its absence. There is perhaps no conclusive evidence that the lax discipline within the Peloponnesian League was attributable to the political diversity which Sparta had tolerated. But the likelihood that such was the case is enhanced by the restoration of discipline under Sparta's leadership as a result of the oligarchic reaction precipitated by its victory over the rebellious allies at Mantinea in 418.[41] Particularly exemplary are the fluctuating policies of Tegea. The collapse of its democracy sharpened its hostility to democratic Mantinea[42] and rendered it insensitive to appeals to join the anti-Spartan Peloponnesian alliance during the Peace of Nicias.[43] But when the oligarchy was overthrown in 370, Tegea lost no time in joining Sparta's opponents.[44] It was largely for constitutional reasons that the Boeotians and Megarians rejected an alliance with anti-Spartan Argos during the Peace of Nicias, since they feared that they would not feel as much at home in an association with the democratic city as they did with oligarchic Sparta.[45] Mantinea, in turn, defected from Sparta to join Argos, not only for reasons of power but also partly out of sympathy for the sister democracy.[46]

At the same time, there is equally good evidence of indifference toward the constitutional question. Constitutional dissimilarity did not, for example, prevent a rapprochement between Corinth and Argos during the Peace of Nicias.[47] Nor did it prevent Sparta's allies from considering, in a moment of bitter disillusionment,[48] the possibility of collaborating with Athens. Sparta too was occasionally guilty of a rather cavalier treatment of the constitutional issue. In 418 it did not hesitate to conclude an alliance with democratic Argos, and in 411 the establishment of the oligarchy of the Four Hundred in Athens did not persuade it to grant terms to the enemy city.

Athens' foreign relations were equally marked by the absence of a consistent pattern. Numerous examples of the decisive importance of the constitutional issue can certainly be found. It may suffice to cite here a few random incidents. The collapse of Athenian power in Central Greece during the First Peloponnesian War can be credited to the oligarchic reaction in that area.[49] Around 460 it was the occurrence of a democratic revolt in Argos which created an atmosphere favorable to an alliance with democratic Athens.[50] Thessaly's break with Athens about 454 was the work of the nobility, while the sympathies of the people continued to incline decidedly toward the Athenian side.[51] After the Athenian defeat at Coronea, the Boeotians created a confederacy having an oligarchic constitution;[52] and in Euboea an anti-democratic reaction went hand in hand with anti-Athenian sentiments.[53] In the late 460's democratic preponderance made possible Megara's integration into the Athenian system.[54] Similarly, Corcyra actively supported Athens during the first war year while the masses had the upper hand.[55] Sympathy more than anything else seems to have induced the democratic cities of Argos, Elis, and Mantinea in 420 to ally themselves with Athens as soon as circumstances permitted.[56] The case of Argos shows particularly clearly the dependence of international commitments on political fluctuations at home.[57] And again, it was the help of the pro-Athenian party that enabled Alcibiades to reconquer Thrace in 409, in return for which he guaranteed his supporters a democratic constitution.[58]

But this rather impressive record too is opposed by considerable evidence to the contrary. Again, we shall make no pretense of completeness. A few examples will suffice to illustrate the point. Constitutional dissimilarity did not preclude long-standing friendly relations between Corinth and Athens, which turned into bitter enmity only when commercial rivalry set off a conflict over Megara shortly before the outbreak of the war.[59] Nor did oligarchic governments prevent Chios, Samos, and Mytilene from maintaining loyalty toward Athens over a long period of time.[60] When Chios defected in 412, the reason was chiefly the seeming destruction of Athenian power rather than constitutional form. It is particularly revealing that the mass defections following the Sicilian disaster were not confined to Athens' oligarchic allies. At that juncture Athens was deserted by a large number of allies for reasons of power, without much apparent consideration for the constitutional issue.

Of particular interest in this connection is the repeatedly mentioned inability of the Four Hundred in 411 to change the course of the war. The constitutional reform of 411 did not strengthen the loyalty of those faltering allies who preferred oligarchic government. The reason no doubt was that the allies' chief interest now that both sides were ruled by oligarchs lay in external independence, and they knew only too well that Sparta alone could break the power of Athens.[61] It is of interest also that the *demos* rarely seems to have interceded to prevent defections from Athens.[62]

To sum up, the leading states certainly were not setting out to nail down a given constitutional type or way of life out of a belief in the superior virtue of their respective systems, nor did they invariably obtain the desired results when they did so. But if the constitutional issue depended mostly on estimates of political expediency, a distinction must be made between the importance which it had for the leading cities and the lesser states. Although considerations of political advantage cannot be ruled out in the case of lesser states, the matter assumed an importance to them which it did not have for Athens and Sparta. In view of the deep social cleavages, external independence frequently was a far less vital question to them than the struggle for power between the oligarchs and the democrats within. In many cases the fear of internal foes vastly outdistanced fear of the external enemy.[63]

For the two contenders, identification with a particular way of life and the political faction championing it was not of equal advantage. In the interwar period Athens had greatly benefited from the subversive effect which the democratic example had upon the status quo. But as the war got underway, positions were reversed. The fact that states identifying themselves with the Athenian cause had gradually been led into subjection gave Sparta a splendid opportunity to make political capital in its turn by portraying the conflict as a war of liberation in behalf of Hellas.[64] There was little Athens could do to counter Sparta's propaganda, which rested on so plausible a basis. But turbulent political conditions worked in Athens' favor. In many instances the dread of the internal enemy caused the democratic forces to look upon the unloved Athenians as protectors against their vengeful oligarchic faction. Because of that fear Athens could maintain discipline within its empire in spite of its general unpopularity. When particularistic tendencies manifested themselves, they normally emanated from the oligarchic party.[65] Only when imperial rule became unbearable or the protector failed to intercede at a critical juncture would the loyalty of the democratic forces and the independence movement become a problem.[66]

A further indication of the pragmatic nature of the issues involved in the war is the alignment of powers. The preference of the mainland states for an alliance with Sparta or neutrality as opposed to association with Athens clearly suggests military reasons. And so does the fact that the islands, with only a few exceptions, were allied with Athens. Evidently its inferiority on land would have given little credence to any promise of effective protection it might have wanted to hold out against assault by land forces. But the superiority of its naval force was living proof of its ability to protect and coerce the insular states.

All this should not obscure the importance which constitutional conformity was to assume as an instrument of war strategy at the hands of Athens and Sparta, as a result of the moralizing tone which bipolarism had infused into foreign policy. But the bipolar structure also generated pressures to engage in this type of warfare. Here, then, lay the paradox of bipolar war. While it encouraged moralizing in foreign policy, the dominant power rationale of bipolarity in actuality relegated the fight for principles to a secondary position.

chapter 6

DOMESTIC POLITICS
AND FOREIGN AFFAIRS

The interdependence of domestic politics and foreign affairs is always of importance for an analysis of international relations, though it has often failed to receive adequate attention. Thucydides is not guilty of such a neglect. The frequent and lengthy discussions which he devotes to internal politics and their impact upon the war can no doubt be explained in large part by his exceptional perspicacity as well as by the characteristic respect of classical thinkers for the complexities of life. But to some extent the answer seems to lie in the very subject of his inquiry, which left him little choice but to take up matters that may at first sight appear to digress from his main subject.

It will be recalled that the scope of the war transcended purely external concerns and that the line between international and civil war, if it had not become obliterated, was greatly blurred. For that reason and because of the growing conviction of the opponents that nothing short of total victory could terminate the war, politics and military affairs had ceased to be clearly separable spheres. Politics in effect had come to be subsidiary to military strategy, which under the circumstances could no longer rely on its own techniques but was forced to fall back on the more subtle and effective methods that politics could provide—such as constitutional conformity, peace offensives, economic and military aid to inveigle allies and neutrals, and political fifth columns and propaganda to subvert enemy morale. This explains the great upheaval caused by the war in the way of life of the people throughout the entire area. The result was a growing difficulty in precisely distinguishing between means and ends.

An entanglement of issues and mutual encroachments of the normally differentiated spheres of internal and external politics can be observed in any major war. But under other more ordinary power configurations, such fusions and confusions are susceptible to some measure of control. In the bipolar struggle they tend to attain such complexity that it becomes impossible either to evade or unravel them. There seems therefore good reason to consider the exceptionally close entanglement of domestic politics and foreign affairs in fifth-century Greece as an adjunct of bipolarism, particularly since this involvement can be observed in both Sparta and Athens. Although there has long been a tendency to consider such entanglement a peculiarity of democracy, it was as unmistakably a characteristic of Sparta's as of Athens' policy, as will be shown a little later on.

The order of priority of the two spheres of politics presents an especially difficult problem. We do not, perhaps cannot, know to what extent foreign policy was the product of the interplay of domestic forces and how basic was the influence exerted by international events upon domestic developments. The origin of the power dualism in Hellas, for example, has more frequently been attributed to the internal clash between the propertied classes and the masses over economic and political issues; however, an equally persuasive argument can be made that it was ultimately caused by the stimulus which the young Athenian democracy received from the Persian War. Certainly no simple and straightline relationship can be detected. But however ambiguous the basic causes may be, it is clear that both spheres had ceased to be autonomous. The management of external affairs had become dependent upon internal political developments to an unusual degree. Conversely, the needs of international strategy were imposing exceptionally stringent limitations upon domestic forces. The most that can be said is that the actual policies of the belligerents were the result of the interaction of both.

IMPACT OF DOMESTIC AFFAIRS ON FOREIGN POLICY

What, then, was the effect of domestic politics on foreign policy? We may first consider whether the constitutional orders of the hostile cities were adaptable to the exigencies of warfare. Unfortunately, Thucydides tells us little about their relative merits. It will therefore be necessary to assemble the piecemeal evidence in order to shed some light on the question.

Sparta's constitutional order had been instrumental in launching Sparta on the road to diplomatic success. As has been seen, the confidence it inspired had caused oligarchic governments in need of protection to rally around Sparta, and this was the basis of its control over most of the Peloponnese. But even outside the Peloponnese, where protection played a less important part, Sparta's political order had traditionally been viewed with admiration. Thucydides too was impressed with Sparta's sustained political stability, which he attributed to the intrinsic virtues of its constitutional order.[1] The clue to its success may well be found in the words he attributes to the Spartan king Archidamus, describing the superior virtue of the Spartans as a combination of courage and wisdom.[2] The apparent implication is that the constitution provided the framework for a commonwealth where such qualities could flourish.

However praiseworthy at the outset, the Spartan system was not immune to corrosion. In the past it had justly earned the epithet of *eunomia* because of its commitment to the rule of law, which formed an agreeable contrast to the practices of both tyrannies and democracies.[3] But over a period of time the principle had been progressively attenuated, and eventually it was common knowledge that Sparta's much-praised *eunomia* was more legendary than real. By the time the Peloponnesian War broke out, it was no more than a party label for oligarchs, signifying their opposition to the democratic principle of *isonomia*.[4] Perhaps all constitutions are subject in some degree to such hazards. The tendency is for constitutional principles to be reduced sooner or later to empty forms and to lend themselves to substantive abuse no matter how admirable they may be in their initial conception. Unless they are adapted to changing social problems and needs, constitutions tend eventually to become fossilized. Although it is impossible to establish a definite causal connection, there seems good reason to attribute the erosion of Sparta's leading position in Hellas in large measure to a constitutional decline.

Sparta's greatest single handicap, the rigidity and timidity of its policy, must also be examined in the light of its constitution. It would of course be possible to charge the stultefying conservatism very simply to an elusive quality such as "national character." But the inherent flaws of the constitutional system seem to provide a more plausible explanation, touching directly upon the bases of the difficulty. In spite of his admiration for what Sparta's constitution had accomplished in earlier times, Thucydides seems to have had mixed feelings concerning its adequacy in the modern era which began with the Persian invasion.[5] The thought is most clearly expressed in Pericles' first speech.[6] The responsibility for Sparta's indecision and inconsistency could largely be traced to the constitutional division of power between royalty and the oligarchs, as well as to the venality of the ephors wielding virtually tyrannical power.[7] The political difficulties were compounded by Sparta's economic backwardness and its fiscal policy of keeping the public treasury at a low level to avoid the corrupting effects of luxuries.[8]

Such institutional handicaps were bad enough, but what ultimately precluded a bold and imaginative foreign policy was the city's stifling intellectual atmosphere. The causes of stagnation were also closely linked to the constitution, which was designed to insure the social and political status quo. The rule of the Spartans over the large indigenous disfranchised population could be secured only through a thorough militarization of Spartan life, subjecting the entire citizenry to barracks discipline. As we saw earlier, the preoccupation with the ever-present threat of an internal upheaval accounted to a large extent for Sparta's failure to consolidate its international leadership during and following the Persian War. A natural disaster, such as an earthquake, would suffice to precipitate a revolt of *perioeci* and *helots*.[9] While such tensions were threatening domestic stability, the Spartans were understandably reluctant to commit substantial military forces to far-flung operations.[10] These handicaps imposed by fear for the stability of a tenuous constitutional status quo persisted during most of the war. The uncertainty of vision which they caused was clearly reflected in Sparta's reluctance to build a navy, the indispensable instrument for asserting its supremacy over Athens.

The purpose behind the constitution could not but have a repressive effect upon the city's creative spirit. Aristotle clearly points out the weakness of Sparta's political order. The Spartan constitution, he said, had "regard to one part of virtue only—the virtue of the soldier which gives victory in war." [11] However, it sorely neglected the development of the virtues required of the good ruler. Hence the Spartans' inability to hold together the empire which their brilliant military exploits had enabled them to acquire, and their failure effectively to play the part of Panhellenic protector when the occasion arose. In short, *eunomia* had produced the admirable virtue of moderation, but at the same time it had generated ignorance and inertia in foreign policy.[12] It is therefore no wonder that fewer and fewer voices should have been heard in its praise, and that Thucydides' *History* should have been replete with derogatory references to Sparta's lethargy.[13]

It is of course possible that these handicaps in foreign policy were offset by advantages derived from an exemplary internal political organization, and we may ask whether and, if so, in what ways the Spartan system was superior to that of other states. Did Sparta produce a unique measure of consistency and rationality in its policy? Were its leaders less corrupt and less subject to the pressure of public opinion than the leaders of democratic states, particularly of Athens? Thucydides' tale shows clearly enough that its constitutional order in fact did not shield Sparta against internal difficulties of the kind which so often played havoc with the Athenian war effort. That is not to say that there was no difference in the frequency with which such embarrassments occurred. It only means that Sparta's policy too had its caprices. The institutional arrangement evidently did not provide dependable guarantees against inconsistency in the conduct of the war. For example, some of the ephors were busily engaged in wrecking the Peace of Nicias at a time when political and strategic interests required its continuation.[14] Evidence of corruption is not lacking either. The case of Pausanias immediately comes to mind.[15] Other examples are the case of Cleomenes, the leader of the hegemonial party, who in face of the Persian menace deserted his city;[16] and that of Lysander, who for reasons of personal interest refused to terminate the war in 407 when it was possible to do so.[17] Thucydides also provides evidence to show that the oligarchic order was not impervious to the influence of public opinion.[18] In fact, it was a change in the faction controlling the government that was responsible for the subversion of the Peace of Nicias.[19]

It can safely be said, then, that Sparta's constitutional order was far from being perfectly adapted to the city's international needs and frequently formed an obstacle to an effective foreign policy. The isolationism it encouraged was anything but conducive to developing the tact and understanding required for a hegemonial power to hold its followers together.[20] There is also reason to doubt that the institutional environment was apt to produce first-rate military leadership. Sparta's successes during the early phases of the war were far from spectacular; and when the picture changed with the fiasco of the Athenian expeditionary force in Sicily, most of the credit was probably due Alcibiades, the defected leader of the Athenian democratic faction, rather than the strategic and political ingenuity of Sparta's own leaders.[21]

The connection between foreign policy and the geographic, economic, and social conditions of a country can be seen more clearly in the case of Athens, whose politics have received a more complete treatment at the hands of Thucydides than those of Sparta. For instance, the development of far-flung interests, we are told, was largely the result of Attica's unfavorable natural conditions, which had made the area appear an unenticing object of conquest and thus permitted its people to turn to trade.[22] A particularly good example of the tie between external and internal politics is furnished by the rather clear division of Athenian opinion on foreign policy, which followed class and party lines generally.[23] Thus the clash of the radical imperialists and those who advocated a more moderate or anti-imperialistic policy paralleled closely that of oligarchs and democrats. The same division existed in relation to the war against the Peloponnesian Confederacy which was popular with the democrats but found little favor with the peasantry and the aristocrats, who had traditionally entertained pro-Spartan tendencies.[24]

The division of opinion can be observed as early as the Persian War. The nobility, supported by rural elements, was the main carrier of the resistance against the invader, whereas the *demos* inclined toward an intra-Hellenic expansionism at the expense of Sparta.[25] The reasons were largely of an economic and sociological nature. To challenge Sparta's leadership by means of naval supremacy, the Athenians had to be willing to make themselves into islanders permanently by abandoning their city's territory and withdrawing to their ships, as they had done temporarily to defeat the Persians at Salamis. The propertyless *demos*, having nothing to lose, apparently was quite willing to put itself on such a footing. However, the well-to-do and the peasants seemed less inclined to abandon their property to seizure and destruction by the enemy.[26] If this, then, was not an acceptable course, the only alternative the propertied classes could support, in view of Athens' inability to match Sparta's land forces, was a policy of friendship with the rival city.

The economic interests of the democratic masses lay in other directions. Overpopulation had brought on a scarcity of goods. The simplest remedy was to relieve the pressure by settling the surplus population abroad and letting the spoils of empire accrue to the benefit of the impoverished masses.[27] Another boon to the Athenian economy was the expansion of the fleet, which created many well-paying jobs.[28] But the enormous expense which that venture entailed could be justified only in terms of an expansionist policy. Conversely, to abandon imperialism would have meant reducing the naval establishment, and this in turn would have brought on economic contraction. Of course there may also have been psychological reasons at the bottom of the imperialist inclinations of the poor. The prospect of suppressing the rich in allied cities no doubt was emotionally satisfying to them, especially when this redounded to their own material advantage.[29]

A close connection thus seemed to exist between the democratic character of the constitution and the nature of the foreign policy which Athens was pursuing. But the establishment of maritime dominion in turn affected the internal power structure, thereby giving an additional impetus to imperialism. The increased political recognition of the *thetes*, who provided the manpower required to propel the instrument of dominion, gave rise to mounting pressures to exploit the city's imperial position.[30] The indigent poor were the main beneficiaries both of the fruits of expansion and of the lavish public works projects at home financed by the contributions of tributary allies.[31] Thus we find on the oligarchic side a combination of anti-democratic, anti-imperialist, anti-war, and pro-Spartan elements,[32] while the masses of the poor were favoring a policy of belligerency and imperialism.

Athens' rise to a leading international position, then, appears to have been closely connected with the democratic development which followed the reforms of Cleisthenes in 508.[33] But there were reasons other than internal pressures which favored the spread of Athenian influence and the growth of Athenian power. We have already alluded to the unsettling effect which the introduction of libertarian institutions had upon people everywhere and to the subversive effect of the very existence of such a system upon governments of a different type. A political arrangement reducing the power of the select few and providing for the effective participation of the masses in public affairs to the extent that they eventually acquired ultimate power of decision seemed an ideal worth fighting for. But the advantages of democracy were not only of the passive type. The great relaxation of authority which it had brought about also did much to build up the city's strength. The wide scope given to individual ingenuity brought to the fore talent of unparalleled quality and quantity.[34] In addition, the city opened itself up to outside influences, adding foreign to native talent.[35] What is more, the enormous intellectual, cultural, and material development rested on a solid political foundation since the participation of the *demos* was providing an exceptionally strong consensus.[36] The extraordinary dedication which the Athenian political order was able to evoke was well illustrated by the continued allegiance of the Athenian forces at Samos to the democracy at a time when the Four Hundred were in control at home.[37]

These assets, inherent in its democratic order, were the source of Athens' great strength. But strength alone was no guarantor of success. The crucial question was whether the Athenian democracy was capable of actions that were both consistent and wise. It certainly had not been incapable of producing first-rate leaders in the past. Thucydides had much praise for Themistocles[38] and, more particularly, for Pericles.[39] What was less certain was the extent to which leaders could count on consistent and sustained support. Admitted to participation in public life, the *demos* was encouraged to take a hand in matters for which it lacked the requisite knowledge and circumspection. In particular, the frequency with which leaders were subjected to undeserved punishment, out of jealousy or unfounded suspicion, could not but have adverse effects upon policy at any time, but was to prove especially disastrous during the war. Even Themistocles was not immune to the vindictiveness of the masses and was ostracized about 471. Pericles himself, who had succeeded in curbing the more extreme vacillations of the democratic process by giving his government a near-monarchical character, found himself the object of the *demos'* ire. Discouraged by the plague and repeated invasions, the *demos* did not hesitate to turn against him in its search for a scapegoat and to try, convict, and sentence him.[40]

A number of ill-conceived and risky ventures undertaken by Athens give further pause. There is not enough evidence to charge the *demos* with responsibility for the inauspicious expeditions against Cyprus and Egypt.[41] But when we turn to the conception and execution of military plans during the war, the role played by the masses stands out more clearly. The Sicilian expedition furnishes a particularly good example. The plan itself, as has been argued earlier, was rational enough. But it was probably not discussed with the open-mindedness and self-criticism which was demanded by the immense scope of so grandiose an enterprise. In fact Thucydides reports that the debate was so dominated by emotions that it was not safe for those opposing it to express their views lest they be suspected of a lack of patriotism.[42] In any event, the venture was sufficiently risky to make the choice of a first-rate leader imperative; it was also necessary to make the utmost effort to provide him with sustained support. But here too the Athenian system of government was wanting. The recall of Alcibiades, who had contrived the plan, shortly after the expedition had set out was very likely based on spurious reasons. Although he was formally charged with participation in sacrilegious activities, the real reason for his recall seems to have been an intrigue instigated by demagogues who did not relish the prospect of a hero's welcome for him if he returned as the conqueror of Sicily.[43]

The removal of an able and enthusiastic leader was bad enough. What was worse was replacing him with the timid Nicias, who had opposed the venture from the outset. The difficulties arising from the untimely and ill-advised change in command were further aggravated by the failure to give needed support to the forces abroad.[44] Still, even if the expedition was to end in failure, disaster could have been avoided. When the hopelessness of the Athenian position had become clear, the main body of their forces might still have been saved by a last-minute withdrawal. However, Nicias, knowing the fickleness of the *demos*, decided against withdrawal for fear that his only reward would be a shameful death at the hands of his countrymen, who would attribute his failure to dishonorable motives.[45]

Nicias' fear was by no means imaginary. Other examples can be cited to show that democratic political maneuvers tended to generate a widespread sense of insecurity among military and political leaders, encouraging either avoidance of risks or commission of treason. A case in point is the desertion of the able general Demosthenes, after his defeat in Aetolia in 426, because of fear of an irate *demos*.[46] And again, Antiphon, whom Thucydides described as one of the most capable Athenians, "being ill-looked upon by the multitude because of his reputation for talent," [47] deemed it hazardous to place himself in the service of his city. A good example of the vengeance visited upon successful or unsuccessful military leaders by the *demos* was the execution of six generals who had been victorious in the battle of Arginusae in 406, because of their alleged failure to rescue shipwrecked Athenian soldiers.[48] Apparently their conviction was based upon the emotions of the aroused masses rather than unimpeachable evidence.

These episodes may suffice to show the hazards inherent in the making of policy under the direct control of the *demos*, limited only by self-imposed restraints and checks resulting from factional strife. It was unlikely that the consistency and intelligence required for rational planning would commonly prevail. But while these handicaps might still be diminished in the planning stage through the influence or control exercised by an intelligent leader, the chief and perhaps uncontrollable problem was the execution of policy. At that point the *demos* was prone to turn on the leader whom it had followed in adopting the plan.

IMPACT OF FOREIGN POLICY ON DOMESTIC AFFAIRS

The influence of external events upon internal affairs is less complex but perhaps also less obvious. However, numerous incidents can be cited to show that such a correlation existed. Since most of the episodes in question have been discussed elsewhere, it will not be necessary to recount them here in detail. Brief references will suffice.

Immediately preceding and during the Peloponnesian War the constitutional forms prevailing in the lesser states often depended, as we saw, on where the fortunes of war had placed them, whether in the Athenian or in the Peloponnesian sphere of influence. And we may remind ourselves that Sparta's own constitutional structure was largely determined by its conquest of Messenia, which condemned its citizens to a difficult military way of life in order to secure the conquest.[49] Sparta's defeat at Pylos in 425 seems to have created problems in regard to the city's social stratification and its power structure, since emancipation was the only meaningful reward that could be given to the *helots* for their willingness to risk their lives in bringing food to the besieged Spartan forces.[50] Occasionally, too, success or failure in battle would cause changes in government. For instance, several defeats suffered in the Hellespont exalted the peace party in 410.[51] By 408 the war party had the upper hand again, and a profound change seems to have occurred in the style of Spartan politics as a result of the definite commitments which the Persian king was now assuming.[52]

Similar observations can be made regarding Athens. A connection between foreign affairs is suggested by the extension of democracy beyond the scope of the Cleisthenic reforms at a time when there was a growing need to defend the empire against internal and external assaults. This necessitated the assignment of top priority to the development of a navy, which had far-reaching consequences for the internal power structure; it opened the door to the participation of the hitherto disfranchised *thetes* in the exercise of political power and thus broke the political monopoly of the well-to-do classes.[53]

The effect of external events upon the internal political process can also be observed in specific instances. Around 470 it was Sparta's support that accounted largely for the success of Cimon's aristocratic party.[54] And a few years later, in 462, Sparta's request that Athenian forces be withdrawn from Ithome proved an involuntary gratuity to the democratic party.[55] The most sweeping effect upon domestic politics was caused by the war itself. In Thucydides' view the great upheaval was ultimately responsible for such crucial developments as the extension of popular self-government, the growing popular distrust of responsible leadership, and the elevation of irresponsible leaders by the masses, in moments of despair as well as overconfidence.[56]

Other examples can be cited. The overthrow of the democracy in Athens in 412–11 can be attributed to the setbacks in the war following the Sicilian disaster.[57] Apparently it was hoped that the Athenian cause could be salvaged by casting aside the democratic constitution, which was believed to be the chief obstacle to receiving Persian aid.[58] The fall of the Four Hundred in turn was brought on not so much by their lack of prudence in managing domestic affairs as by the Athenian defeat in Eretria.[59] Similarly, the government of the Five Thousand, which in Thucydides' opinion rested on the best constitution Athens had had in his time, came to a quick end after the crushing victory of the Athenians at Cyzicus, which revived the self-confidence of the more radically inclined seamen.[60] To continue the list: the defeat at Ephesus in 407 was followed by the abolition of the office of supreme commander held by Alcibiades, whose boundless ambition had made him widely suspect.[61] Again, the news of the final defeat at Aegospotami strengthened the war party in Athens, which was in the throes of an overpowering fear of retribution for its misdeeds during the war, and it was not until the radicals were turned out that peace could be made.[62] More instances could be given, but the incidents cited may suffice to illustrate the point which concerns us here.

DISINTEGRATION OF THE ETHOS

The ineptitudes of the belligerent governments and their easy susceptibility to despair cannot be attributed to personal shortcomings and institutional inadequacies alone. The intensity and persistence of the predicaments facing the warring peoples had deeper causes. Throughout Thucydides' *History* we are reminded of the calamities and anguish springing from the social disintegration of the Greek states and the moral degradation which accompanied it. Thucydides gives a vivid description of the upheaval in his account of the revolution in Corcyra, which in its essential points strikingly resembles the demoralization caused by the plague in Athens. The specific example here serves to illustrate a general condition. Inasmuch as Thucydides informs us that the convulsion eventually was to grip the entire Hellenic world,[63] his presentation must be accepted as a general exposition of the social and moral conditions throughout Greece, without regard to political form. He exempts neither Sparta nor other oligarchies explicitly or implicitly. Although there is little evidence of any factional strife of great consequence in Sparta during the war, there are indications that it too succumbed to the relativization of values which stands out more clearly in the case of the democracies. It seems in fact that its politics came to resemble more closely those of Athens after the death of Brasidas—as the elevation of Lysander, a kind of counterpart of the Athenian demagogues, would suggest.[64] There also is no indication that Thucydides intended to give a clean bill of health to oligarchs in general. It suffices to recall his lurid description of the reign of the Four Hundred as well as the ready acquiescence of most of the Athenian oligarchs to their city's imperialistic policy.

The social dissolution had its early beginnings in the acrimony of the class struggle between the oligarchs and the democrats. The consequent displacement of the state as the highest focus of allegiance by particularistic interests necessarily resulted in the loss of a common purpose, common norms, modes of thought, and conceptions of the world. The state itself in effect became the playball of particularistic and selfish interests.[65] In such a context, characterized by the evaporation of a common sense, social relations must dissolve, and generally applicable ethical postulates cease to be relevant. This is the essence of the picture Thucydides paints. Such customary and natural obligations as those toward family and friends, he relates, were no longer acknowledged.[66] The only association able effectively to claim loyalty was the political party. But it was not only social values that were destroyed in the process. Ultimately transcendental values were rejected as well to clear the way for the sanctification of material success.

The moral relativism was to attack the very foundations of the societies that embraced it. Questions of truth and justice, having become irrelevant, could no longer safely be raised. The objective standard of the vanishing *ethos* was replaced by the wholly subjective standard of opinion. Consequently, demands for justice, which can never be totally suppressed, were quickly silenced; and bad laws, unrelated to any higher standards than the interest of the power holders, were justified in terms of an alleged need for stability and security. Boisterous aggressiveness was rewarded as patriotism and prudent restraint denounced as cowardice.

The true magnitude of the social dissolution can be gauged from the confusion of language and concepts which Thucydides describes. It was no coincidence that people should have become obsessed with the desire to conceal their more sinister purposes and to cover up real clashes of interest and real divergences of outlook. They tried to attain their objectives by resorting to a form of "double-think" and "newspeak." Identical words no longer had the same meaning when employed by partisans of different persuasions, and identical facts and situations were referred to by different names. When such sophistries became general practice, they produced effects that may not have been foreseen. The conceptual confusion was more than a mere symptom of the corrosion which had already attacked the social foundations. It had a dynamics of its own causing further social disintegration. The loss of precise and generally accepted meanings was bound to preclude any purposeful communication. The resulting destruction of a rudimentary common sense was to spell the end of the social consensus.

The obliteration of objective standards of morality greatly aided factional leaders in the attainment of their ends. The sense of insecurity and mutual distrust following the substitution of subjective values for moral precepts enabled them to enlist the support of the timid and the undecided. Frontal assaults on reason and knowledge, of which Thucydides gives an example in Cleon's speech,[67] were ideally suited to satisfy the anti-intellectual longings of the masses, who were stirred less by logical arguments than by appeals to their emotions. Thus released from the obligations of custom and morality, they were prepared to accept the demagogue's interest as the sole canon of truth, wisdom, and justice.

In such an atmosphere friend-enemy relations would replace the precepts of morality as the source of social norms. What mattered was to jump on the bandwagon of the powerful. Whoever failed to do so had thereby relegated himself to the category of enemy and was condemned to social and political, if not physical, obliteration.[68]

The evidence which Thucydides provides for the practical effects of the social and moral dissolution pertains mostly to Athens. One of his main purposes throughout was to show how Athens lost the war, despite its good prospects, as a result of internal disorder. This could in part be attributed to the Athenian constitution, which, to be sure, had created an impressive consensus and maintained a high level of morale as long as crises did not impose a greater strain than the *demos* was able to bear. But it had also produced an atmosphere conducive to the promotion of selfish ends. It is no wonder that the lower classes, at last come into their own politically, should have wanted to satisfy their longings for tangible material improvements. Thus absorbed in the task of achieving material progress, they had little concern for moral distinctions. Popular passions caused the constructive potentialities of the energies released by the democratic reforms to deteriorate into a purposeless and self-perpetuating activism. Unfortunately, such a preoccupation with material self-improvement was designed to estrange the citizen from the concerns of the city as a whole and shift his allegiance to an association of a lower order, the faction.

To be sure, the Athenian constitution was not lacking in safeguards against such corrosive tendencies. The possibility of corruption was minimized by the accountability of magistrates. The antidote against the disruptive effects of factionalism was the institution of ostracism, through which defeated political leaders could be removed from the scene for extended periods. However, such provisions proved of little value under the strains of war. They were aimed only at the symptoms and did not strike at the root of the problem. They did not curb the materialistic spirit which the constitution had fostered. The conciliatory effect which war often has on internal dissension did not materialize in this particular war. On the contrary, by adding a further dimension to the international contest in the form of civil war, the bipolar conflict split even wider a society already poisoned by hatreds.

The Athenian democracy could maintain a relatively high standard of public morality while Pericles held the reins. A happy combination of political ability with patriotism and immunity to corruption was what made him a great leader. But such men are rare, and it is not surprising that in the absence of adequate constitutional restraints standards should have deteriorated after his death. With his demise leadership passed to a line of demagogues bent on exploiting their popularity with the masses for their own gain.[69] Even Alcibiades, by far the brightest light in that uninspiring procession, held out little promise. Although equal to Pericles in ability and nobility of birth, he was sorely lacking in patriotism and moral standards, the attributes of greatness which Pericles had possessed in abundance.[70] It is true that Pericles probably shared a goodly measure of responsibility for preparing the way for his city's decline. Although it is unlikely that he had anything to do with the introduction of the reforms of 462–61, he supported them in his efforts to defeat the Cimonian faction[71] and thereby committed himself to a policy of continuous liberalization. Quite possibly Pericles did not have much choice in the matter. Once the populist forces had been unleashed through the reforms of Cleisthenes, the pressure exerted by them may have become too strong to be reversed or arrested by the time Pericles was entering the arena.

The demagogues who followed Pericles differed from their great predecessor in their indifference toward genuinely political ends. It was not the welfare of the *polis* that concerned them but the success of the faction they were leading. Instead of desiring power for the attainment of higher common goals, they looked upon its seizure as an end in itself, at times as the only means of self-preservation but usually for self-gratification and profit.[72]

The relativization of moral standards and the leadership problem it created had far-reaching consequences in foreign policy and the conduct of the war. The most conspicuous weakness of the leaders of post-Periclean Athens was their lack of moderation. Thucydides repeatedly points to the inability of the demagogues to strike a workable balance. The primacy of domestic politics over foreign affairs in the thinking of factional leaders frequently produced policies that either were at variance with strategic requirements or were lacking in the foresight which the seriousness of the situation demanded. Thucydides evidently did not think that from the military and economic point of view the defeat of Athens was a matter of necessity. He quite clearly attributed it to mistakes which might have been avoided under a better ordered political system.[73]

One cannot quarrel on principle with Thucydides' contention. Unfortunately the question as to specifically when moderation was and when it was not appropriate is considerably more problematic. There are of course some instances that are clear and simple to decide. The atrocities committed against the people of warring and neutral states *qua* human beings would not then and will not today be accepted by civilized men on the grounds of military necessity or reason of state. In reading the numerous episodes of man's inhumanity to man cited by Thucydides—Mytilene, Plataea, Scione, Torone, Melos, Mycalessus, Syracuse—it is impossible to find any basis for exculpation. These instances, implicating Greeks and barbarians, Dorians and Ionians, Athenians, Spartans, and Sicilian Greeks, reflect and probably were intended to reflect the universality of the moral decline of the period. One may also, without any great difficulty, regard as imprudent the insistence of the *demos* that Cleon make good his boast that he would bring the Spartans besieged at Pylos to Athens within twenty days. The fact that he succeeded in what appeared to be a hopeless enterprise in no way detracts from the folly of the decision and of the spirit in which it was made.[74]

We are faced with far more difficult problems when trying to decide whether the war could have been avoided, whether imperialism was susceptible to limitation, or whether Athens should and could have respected the neutrality of Melos. The difficulty derives from the fact that power can never be contained by simple and clearcut moral maxims. Frequently the only possible choice available to statesmen is between several evils, some greater and some smaller. Justice must often yield to the need for order. The odium of power must be borne because of the nobility of its objects, Pericles allegedly informed his countrymen.[75] The basis of the dilemma lies in the rudimentary nature of the international community. In the absence of central institutions resting on consensus, the order, such as it is, must necessarily be determined by the strongest power. In such an order self-reliance alone can insure security. The need for self-reliance is especially great under bipolar conditions when the scope for maneuver and the possibility of depending on allied aid is greatly reduced.

It is therefore necessary to distinguish between situations in which the human agent has a reasonable choice and those in which a reasonable choice is denied him by circumstances beyond his control; that is, we must distinguish between human responsibility and the fatality inherent in power itself. Such a distinction is not easy to make. As for the outbreak of the war, it was Pericles who refused to take the steps required to avoid it. Under the circumstances he evidently considered war inevitable, and Thucydides seems to have shared his view. As for his successors, they did not deviate in essence from the main lines of his policy. As we saw in an earlier chapter, Cleon acted entirely in Pericles' sense in enforcing imperial discipline, and so did Alcibiades in refusing to limit expansion to the existing boundaries of the empire. What Pericles would not have condoned was the death sentence which Cleon pronounced upon the people of Mytilene or Alcibiades' consuming ambition in fixing his sights upon the far corners of the world well beyond Sicily.

The climax of Thucydides' presentation of the dilemma of power is reached with the Melian dialogue. Here the overriding force of power considerations is coldly stated, without any attempt to embellish or to cover up. But although the reader's moral indignation is easily aroused, it is far from clear upon reflection how the episode is to be interpreted. Thucydides offers no comment, nor does he explicitly condemn the Athenians for acting as they did. Yet he has nothing to say in their defense but lets their argument speak for itself. What, then, is the lesson to be learned; and if the Athenian action was worthy of censure, what is it that merits condemnation? It cannot have been the brutal treatment of the Melians, which had not as yet taken place and has no part in the dialogue. There also was nothing new in the argument of the Athenian envoys that the existence of a neutral island was a strategic hazard to the mistress of the sea. The reasoning follows rather closely the line customarily taken by the Athenians in justifying their imperialism. Historical accident rather than conscious design had given rise to the empire. Once it was a fact, considerations of security left them no choice but to defend it, even if this meant renewed encroachments upon the rights of others. The status of Melos had a definite bearing on Athens' imperial defense. Its possession would bring substantial strategic advantages. Its continued neutrality would undermine the prestige of Athenian naval power, which in the eyes of the world either was not able or did not dare to incorporate the island into its imperial system. If viewed from such a perspective, the rationale of the conquest of Melos in fact was not essentially different from the reasons underlying the attack on Sicily a few years later. Yet Thucydides did not regard the plan for the Sicilian expedition as either irrational or reprehensible, nor is his narrative designed to produce the same sense of indignation as does the Melos episode.

The question whether Melos actually was neutral at the time or whether it had been a tributary ally of Athens and was now reneging on its obligation, which has formed the subject of a good many recent scholarly discussions, need not here detain us. Thucydides evidently intended his treatment of the episode as a paradigm exhibiting a particular predicament characteristic of the politics of the period. There seems no reason why we should not accept it in that spirit for the present purpose. The point at issue between the Athenians and the Melians is the needs of power overriding all other considerations, and the only canons of relevancy for the debate are political. The Melians themselves raise the moral problem only at the outset, and, when the Athenians reject such objections as unfit subjects for rational discourse, they confine their discussion to the terms stated by their adversaries; that is, they agree to argue their case wholly in terms of expediency. No further attempt is seriously made to invoke moral sanctions.[76]

Even if full allowance is made for the antinomy of power, two disturbing facets remain nevertheless, and these may have been the causes of Thucydides' perturbation. The fact that power is governed by laws of its own and defies containment by the precepts of ordinary morality does not mean that the exercise of power is wholly absolved from moral obligation. Even granted that the Athenians in the given conditions had no choice but to integrate neutral Melos into their imperial system, this did not give political leaders *carte blanche* to dismiss moral questions as irrelevant. To raise the moral issue may not mean positively to limit power, but it may have the effect of restraining excesses and thus preventing the dehumanization of those who wield it. The rigid exclusion of moral concerns was to remove the possibility that moderation and humaneness would prevail.

The second disconcerting aspect is the method of stating the autonomy of power as a general proposition that can be applied mechanically without any thought to man's moral nature and to the specific circumstances of the given situation.[77] Politics, in its best and true sense, means meeting the needs of power through courses of action that are practically possible and justifiable before the eyes of the civilized world. Where the "laws of politics" are mechanized through a static formula, politics become brutalized, and the possibility of civilized conduct is left to chance. In sum, it was not the seizure of Melos as such that could be objected to. Rather, what must arouse moral sensibilities is the manner in which it was done—the insensitivity to the "odium of power," the thoughtless compliance with political needs without remorse or compassion, which the Melian dialogue reveals. This very possibly is what Thucydides intended to express in his picture of the demoralization of his time.[78]

It is unlikely that one great leader such as Pericles, however overtowering his stature, could have stemmed the moral decline of his city. One may perhaps agree with Thucydides that he could have led Athens to victory, but it is hard to imagine that he could have curbed his countrymen's greed and ambition. Nevertheless, his high moral qualities combined with his exceptional political ability would very likely have been a restraining influence and prevented warfare from sinking to the moral depth it did.[79] Moderation, which was Pericles' supreme political principle, was abandoned by his successors, who did not recognize any standards transcending the moral climate of the moment and who abandoned themselves to self-promotion and self-gratification without concern for the basic dictates of humanity.

chapter 7

RETROSPECT
AND AFTERMATH

FAILURE OF THE CONTESTANTS

It remains to summarize the chief points hitherto made. Perhaps the best way to do this will be to reduce the more egregious blunders of the contestants to their most basic terms. The principal question which comes to mind is the role played by the deficient statesmanship of Athens and Sparta. If it was the pressures emanating from the bipolar distribution of power rather than the preference of human agents that had brought on the war, and which during the war had greatly reduced the scope of free choice, can one fairly attribute the causes of the disaster either to the lack of moderation of the Athenians or to the passivity of the Spartans?

It may be objected that in the last analysis the war was futile, in that Sparta did not derive any long-range benefits from its victory. But even if this objection be granted, does it prove that the opponents had it within their power to avoid war? States are not normally deterred from going to war, especially when obsessed by irreducible anxieties over their security, by the knowledge that they are not likely to incur material or political gains of any consequence. Pericles, to be sure, was not without responsibility in precipitating the war, and most of his contemporaries seem to have laid the blame squarely upon him. However, Thucydides judged him far more charitably. Although he concedes that Pericles wanted war, in his judgment he wanted it only because the actual combination of circumstances left no room for an alternate course of action.

If one wants to push the argument further, one may ask what would have happened had Athens and Sparta steadfastly refused to go to war. The question obviously is purely hypothetical. The period was not pervaded by pacifist ideologies, nor did avoidance of war at the price of appeasement have any foundation in the *ethos* of the Greeks. But assuming that Athens had yielded to Sparta's demands in order to avoid war, pressure would very likely have been increased and eventually resulted in its reduction. Had Sparta refused to go to war no matter what the circumstances, Athenian power no doubt would have grown until it became an irreducible threat to Sparta's security. But what if both sides had been equally determined to avoid war while insuring mutual containment? The answer lies in the failure of the fifteen years' peace from 446 to 431, which was intended to insure such a state of affairs.

Thucydides refrained from condemning or absolving either side and from blaming the great misfortune on specific individuals or states. It is impossible to say with any assurance that he favored either Athens or Sparta. He does not permit himself expressions of partiality to the belligerents or to a particular type of political organization. It evidently was his desire to unfold before the reader's eye the full complexity of the predicament that was confronting the Greek world. Astutely aware that the magnitude of the problems often eluded the possibility of human control, he condemned neither side for making war or for subjecting their fellow Greeks to imperial rule.

The fact that circumstances had greatly reduced the area of free choice and were frequently forcing the participants into courses of action which they might not have chosen had the pressures been less overwhelming does not of course mean that Sparta's victory was a historical necessity or that it could have been anticipated. On the contrary, Athens' prospects appeared considerably brighter at the outset than Sparta's. If Athens failed nevertheless, the explanation is to be found in faulty statesmanship.

Athens, as we saw, had displayed a boundless activity, attributable both to its naval expansion and its democratic institutions, which produced unique military strength and impressive cultural achievements. But if Athens was to reap the full benefit of these advantages, it was in particular need of restraint lest it become the victim of overextension. This the Athenian institutions failed to provide. While the democratic constitution had generated a high level of morale, it could not maintain moral steadiness under the strain imposed by the protracted war.

The record indicates that Athens' defeat was largely the result of an inability to keep its own house in order. Overextension and dissipation of power, a propensity to rash decisions in situations requiring circumspect action, oscillations between indecision and extremism, and distrust of its leaders stand out as the immediate causes of the city's decline. The difficulties arising from the intellectual and moral ambivalence of the masses, who ultimately charted the course of Athenian policy, were aggravated by the factional hatred dividing the citizenry. This rather than Sparta's superior virtue decided the war.[1]

Whether Athens would have fared better under a different form of government, we can only conjecture. Any temptation to answer affirmatively must be tempered by Thucydides' apparent refusal to confine his observations on the social and moral disintegration to Athens or to democratic states. As far as one can tell, he was describing a condition prevailing throughout Greece, irrespective of forms of government. But events might perhaps have taken a different turn had Athens been able to devise more adequate imperial institutions and to contain its imperialist drive. In failing to placate autonomist resentments among its allies by taking them into partnership and devising democratic institutions for the empire, Athens deprived itself of an important strategic asset and added to the general demoralization of warfare.

The containment of expansion was a more difficult problem, as we have seen. But even so moderation was necessary. In fact, the need was perhaps all the greater because up to a point strategic requirements favored expansionism. Pericles had clearly foreseen both the need and the difficulty of self-restraint, but his warning was ignored by his successors. In short, the pitfalls of Athenian policy consisted less in imperialism as such than in the inability to apply the restraints which prudence demanded. How much responsibility must be borne by defective institutions and how much by the moral climate of the period, it is impossible to say. The two are not clearly separable spheres.

The fact that Sparta was victorious is no necessary proof of the superiority of its political system. Having a government vastly more stable than that of Athens was an undeniable asset. But such advantage could compensate neither for strategic deficiencies nor for political handicaps inherent in stability. Sparta's disabilities are succinctly summarized in a speech of Archidamus, one of the Spartan kings.[2] Sparta, he contended, was not prepared for war with a people having "an extraordinary familiarity with the sea," being grossly deficient in the most important requisites—ships and money. Moreover, Sparta's isolationist policy prior to the war had been neglectful of the need for extra-Peloponnesian allies, whose contributions could not be dispensed with in a war of such magnitude as the one that was then imminent. Under their constitutional order the Spartans had developed the admirable quality of wise moderation, but their foreign policy was marked by inertia. They were charged in rather bitter terms by the Corinthian allies with timidity, rigidity, and conservatism.[3] It must of course be admitted that the Corinthians probably were here resorting to a rhetorical device to stir the Spartans into action. Nevertheless, Sparta's inertia was so widely recognized as to earn the Spartans as well as the pro-Spartan factions in other states the epithet of *apragmones,* a not altogether flattering term to characterize their undue cautiousness.[4]

The conduct of the war similarly reflected Sparta's lack of flexibility and imagination. Almost to the end, its strategy consisted chiefly in the invasion of enemy territory by land forces. No doubt the fortification of Decelea and its use as a base from which to undertake forages into Attic territory in the latter phase of the war were effective in harrassing the Athenians. But although Thucydides regarded this strategy as one of the principal causes of Athens' ruin,[5] it seems doubtful that it would have led Sparta to success had it not been for Athenian blunders and for the construction of a navy made possible by the financial contributions of the Persian king.

Of the deficiencies which hamstrung the operations of both parties no doubt some might have been obviated or at least mitigated. But it is impossible to overlook the fact that many of the more serious predicaments resulted from the bipolar power structure and thus were to some extent impervious to manipulation by human agents. Under the circumstances Sparta had little choice but to rally to the defense of the status quo, even if this implied commitment to a conservative role which left little room for initiative and maneuver. The Athenians were similarly limited in their choices by the force of circumstances. In the given conditions their own security depended entirely on the security of their empire, whose defense precluded a static policy. Their relentless drive toward ever greater and more hazardous ventures was their ruin.

THE AFTERMATH

With the Spartan victory at Aegospotami and the subsequent surrender of Athens, our story comes to an end. The bipolar stalemate had been resolved and Sparta left in virtual control of Hellas. However, some questions come to mind bearing upon the problem at hand, which make it appear worthwhile to pursue developments a little further.

The problem of the balance of power, which had plagued the Hellenic world for approximately sixty years, had been eliminated for the moment. But how was the new balance of power, which was to arise within a decade, to shape up? Had Sparta given any thought to long-range developments or had it been so preoccupied by the immediate objectives of the war to consider the question of the postwar order as too remote to merit attention? It was hardly

to be expected, even after the opponent had surrendered unconditionally, that the status quo, which Sparta had risked so much
to restore, could be preserved in perpetuity.

In looking at the aftermath, the most immediate surprise is
Sparta's magnanimity toward its defeated opponent. Its failure to
destroy Athenian power has been alternately acclaimed as political
wisdom and denounced as a serious blunder. Neither view is entirely satisfactory. It should be recalled that, in spite of Athens'
unconditional surrender, the victory was not decisive. It had not
been the result of Sparta's superior strength but was made possible
only through sustained Persian aid. Actually Sparta was no less
exhausted than its vanquished enemy and, notwithstanding its
temporary supremacy in Hellas, far from capable of assuming the
obligations which its leadership implied. It was unlikely that Sparta
would be able to assert its supremacy over the ambitious and still
powerful Corinthians and Thebans for any length of time. This
may explain the consideration it was showing Athens. Although its
military supremacy was generally acknowledged at the end of the
war, its war-weariness and essential weakness soon became apparent.
To be sure, its power was adequate to ward off threats emanating
from an alliance of its rivals under Athenian leadership, but it
lacked the stamina to follow up its victories.

Another and equally serious problem was the aspirations of the
Persian king. After the defeat of its fleet in 394 at the hands of
the Athenians and the Persians, Sparta was powerless to prevent
him from imposing his will upon the Hellenic world and from
assuming the long-contested jurisdiction over the Ionian cities. The
King's Peace of 386 provided Sparta with a last opportunity for
virtually absolute domination of the Greek mainland and the
Aegean islands. However, that last fling proved to be of short
duration. Sparta was no match for the rising power of Thebes,
and with the battle of Leuctra in 371 Epaminondas definitively
broke Sparta's power. Even when the King's Peace was renewed
shortly thereafter, Sparta's tyrannical rule over the Greeks had
come to an end. Not only did it have to suffer repeated invasions
of the Peloponnese by Epaminondas in the following years, but it

was also powerless to prevent the division of the Peloponnese into two hostile parts.

It might of course be wondered whether—if Sparta proved both impotent and incompetent—leadership might not have passed to some other Greek state. Actually two likely candidates were on the scene. One was Athens, whose power was once again on the rise as a result of Sparta's leniency and an understanding with the Persian king; and several attempts to restore its empire were in fact made. However, all hopes that such a development might materialize were soon dashed. The great war had left it too exhausted politically and financially to follow through the promising beginnings. The other candidate was Thebes. Its rise was impressive but short-lived. While capable of dealing with either Athens or Sparta alone, it lacked the strength to overcome their combined power. Nor was it a match for the naval power of the Persian king.

Sparta's failure to recapture effective leadership among the Hellenic states was not only due to its inadequacies in the military realm but even more to the persistence of fundamental problems that were all-Greek in scope. Although the war had resolved the immediate problem of the international distribution of power, it had not restored Greek society to social and moral health. The lessening of the class struggle which occurred immediately after the war was of short duration, and after the brief interlude revolutions and economic crises continued unabashed. Sparta was not impervious to the effects of such continuous upheavals. The wisdom and integrity which had been the motto of its crusade against Athens soon were to reveal themselves as empty boasts. Now that it was the undisputed master of Greece, Sparta was no more capable than Athens had previously been of coping with the problems created by the machinations of ambitious and corrupt leaders.

The outstanding example is the case of Lysander, the victor of Aegospotami. Hardly had Athens been defeated before he used his city's unique power position to build a personal hegemony to serve his interests and satisfy his pride. All over the defunct Attic empire he established oligarchic governments in the form of so-called decarchies, clearing the path for a reign of carpetbaggers which surpassed the worst abuses of Athenian rule. Little attention was paid to the wishes of the people. Democracies were abolished everywhere and a reign of terror introduced. *Harmosts* were left in all cities visited by Lysander. The system was soon to collapse. Not even in Athens, where a political purge had taken place following the collapse, could the oligarchs maintain a superficial measure of order for any length of time. Bitter discord and bloody fighting necessitated the restoration of democracy in the defeated city as early as 403. It is understandable enough that the Spartans should have felt the need for curbing as ambitious and self-indulgent a leader as Lysander. But to do so at a time when his military and political genius was sorely needed for the imminent showdown with Persia is highly reminiscent of the earlier practices of the Athenian democracy. Just as Athens had deprived itself of Alcibiades' genius at a crucial moment, Sparta now cast aside the one man who might have saved the day in order to placate his less capable rivals.[6]

The eclipse of Sparta's moderation, which had once been its pride and its boast, was mirrored in the espousal of an imperialism no less extreme than that practiced by the Athenians at an earlier time. The temptations of luxury, flattery, gain, and conquest were too great to resist. One is reminded of the prophecy of the Athenians before the commencement of the war, which Thucydides reports in the following words:

If you were to succeed in overthrowing us and in taking our place, you would speedily lose the popularity with which fear of us has invested you, if your policy of today is at all to tally with the sample that you gave of it during the brief period of your command against the Mede. Not only is your life at home regulated by rules and institutions incompatible with those of others, but your citizens abroad act neither on these rules nor on those which are recognized by the rest of Hellas.[7]

The initial moderate objective of consolidating control over the Peloponnese gave way during the King's Peace to the extension of dominion over virtually all of Hellas as far as it was not preempted by the king. The methods used to attain that objective were hardly more enlightened than those of the Athenian imperialists had been. Not only was Sparta equally ruthless in exacting contributions, but the degree of centralization it imposed even exceeded that which had prevailed in the Athenian empire.

The Spartan dilemma was aggravated by the failure to reform its traditional institutions, which proved inadequate to meet the demands of the postwar world. They stubbornly persisted in their hostility to innovation and in adhering to an outdated political and economic order. The social and moral dissolution was permitted to proceed apace; and, just as in Athens, class interests came to displace the concerns of the *polis* and success, moral standards. The resulting lack of vitality was hardly designed to fortify Sparta against the two-fold threat which emanated from the restive *helots* within and the resentful Greeks without.

The Peloponnesian War did not resolve the basic problems threatening Greek society. Relations among the Greek states remained in grave disarray. The real beneficiary was the Persian king. In depending for its victory on his help Sparta had left the Greek world exposed to Persian ambitions. Perhaps the Greeks were still strong enough to stave off the Persians before Sparta's defeat at Leuctra. But inability to overcome their disunity left them at the mercy of a weak and internally torn enemy.

The change in the power constellation, resulting from the defeat of Athens, implied no appreciable improvement for any part of the Greek world. The aggressive and offensive character of Sparta's leadership as well as its short duration did not provide the basis for a recovery of Greece under a universal peace. Instead of producing a monocentric power system, the war had ended in the defeat of one side and the exhaustion of the other. What emerged was a new multiple balance of power composed of weak units fighting each other without purpose or political vision. Their petty quarrels prevented political combinations on a larger scale and left the area exposed to the hazards of external attack. They succumbed to the Macedonian onslought at Chaeronea in 338. Only after the loss of their independence was unity at last established among the Greek states under the *aegis* of the semi-barbarians of the North.

NOTES

CHAPTER ONE

1   *Cf.* Wilhelm Schmid and Otto Stählin, *Geschichte der Griechischen Litera-tur* (Munich, 1948), V, Second Half, Part 2, 29; hereinafter cited as Schmid and Stählin, *Griechische Literatur.* Also see Henrik Samuel Nyberg, "Das Reich der Achämeniden," in Fritz Valjavec (ed.), *Historia Mundi* (10 vols.; Bern, 1954), III, 87.

2   Thuc., 1.88. See also Thuc., 1.86.

3   Thuc., 8.43.

4   *Hellenica,* 1.6.

5   Thuc., 1.128.

6   Thuc., 1.137–38.

7   Thuc., 1.82; 1.137; 2.7; 2.8.

8   *Cf.* Georg Busolt, *Griechische Geschichte bis zur Schlacht bei Chaeroneia* (3 vols.; Gotha, 1893–1904), Vol. III, Pt. 2 (1904), 958–60.

9   A. W. Gomme, *A Historical Commentary on Thucydides* (3 vols.; Oxford, 1945 and 1956), I, 202, 214; hereinafter cited as Gomme, *Commentary.* See also Thuc., 2.7. and 2.102.

10   Thuc., 6.17–18; 6.88; 7.27; 7.29.

11   Thuc., 8.81.

12   Thuc., 8.5; 8.28; 8.31; 8.80; 8.81; 8.83.

13   Thuc., 4.50.

14   Thuc., 8.18; 8.37; 8.57.

15   Thuc., 8.78; 8.83; 8.99.

16   Thuc., 8.47 ff.; 8.56; 8.81.

17   Thuc., 8.81–82.

18   Thuc., 8.46.

19   *Cf.* Schmid and Stählin, *Griechische Literatur,* V, ii, 2, 105.

20   Thuc., 2.68; 2.80; 4.124; 5.83; 7.27; 7.29; 7.42.

21   *Cf.* Eduard Schwartz, *Das Geschichtswerk des Thukydides* (2nd ed.;

Bonn, 1929), 177–78.

22 Thuc., 5.26.

23 Thuc., 1.1; 5.26; 8.96.5.

24 Thuc., 1.100–101.

25 Thuc., 1.103.

26 Thuc., 1.95.1.

27 Thuc., 8.2.

28 Thuc., 2.27.

29 Thuc., 5.14.

30 Brasidas' appeals for the cooperation of the Acanthians did not, for example, contain a solitary reference to loyalties of blood and history. Thuc., 4.84.

31 Thuc., 4.85 ff.

32 Thuc., 4.61.2–3.

33 Thuc., 1.23.6.

34 Thuc., 1.1.2.

35 Gomme, *Commentary*, I, 91.

36 Thuc., 1.1; 1.18; 2.12.

37 Thuc., 2.8.

38 Thuc., 1.89–117.

39 Thuc., 1.97.2.

40 Thuc., 1.18.

41 Thuc., 2.62.

42 Thuc., 1.75.4; 1.86.

43 Thuc., 1.122; 1.123.1.

44 Thuc., 1.77.6.

45 John H. Finley, Jr., has persuasively argued that Thucydides' views in fact express the prevalent attitudes of his time, in Finley, "Euripides and Thucydides," *Harvard Studies in Classical Philology*, XLIX (1938), 23–68. See also H. Patzer, *Das Problem der Geschichtsschreibung des Thukydides und die thukydideische Frage* (Berlin, 1937), 17–20.

46 Thuc., 4.20.

47 Thuc., 8.2.

CHAPTER TWO

1 Thuc., 1.97–117.

2 *Cf.* J. A. O. Larsen, "The Constitution of the Peloponnesian League," *Classical Philology*, XXVIII (1933), 257–76; XXIX (1934), 1–19.

3 Fritz Schachermeyr, "Geschichte der Hellenen bis 356," in Fritz Valjavec (ed.), *Historia Mundi* (10 vols.; Bern, 1954), III, 149–50.

4 *Cf.* J. A. O. Larsen, "The Constitution of the Peloponnesian League," 267.

5 *Cf.* Georg Busolt, *Griechische Geschichte bis zur Schlacht bei Chaeroneia* (3 vols.; Gotha, 1893–1904), I (1893), 710.

6 J. A. O. Larsen, "Federation for Peace in Ancient Greece," *Classical Philology*, XXXIX (1944), 150.

7 N. G. L. Hammond, *A History of Greece to 322 B.C.* (Oxford, 1959), 223; hereinafter cited as Hammond, *History*.

8 *Cf.* P. A. Brunt, "The Hellenic League against Persia," *Historia. Zeitschrift für alte Geschichte*, II (1953), 135–63.

9 J. A. O. Larsen, "The Constitution and Original Purpose of the Delian League," *Harvard Studies in Classical Philology*, LI (1940), 175ff. See also his articles in *Classical Philology*, XXVIII (1933) and *Classical Philology*, XXXIX (1944), cited in n. 2 and 6, *supra*.

10 Thuc., 1.3.4.

11 Busolt, *Griechische Geschichte*, II (1895), 541–42.

12 Herodotus, 5.49–51; 5.97.

13 Busolt, *Griechische Geschichte*, II, 504.

14 *Cf.* Georg Busolt, *Die Lakedaimonier und ihre Bundesgenossen* (Leipzig, 1878), I, 394–96; hereinafter cited as Busolt, *Lakedaimonier*. See also Thuc., 1.92. and Herodotus, 5.21ff.; 6.21; 6.49ff.; 6.106; 6.120; 9.60.

15 Thuc., 1.135.

16 Thuc., 1.102.

17 It is so argued by Plutarch, *Cimon*, 16–17.

18 *Cf.* Hammond, *History*, 226ff.

19 Herodotus, 7.132.

20 Busolt, *Griechische Geschichte*, Vol. III, Pt. 1 (1897), 68ff.

21 *Cf.* Hammond, *History*, 246.

22 Herodotus, 8.142.

23 Busolt, *Lakedaimonier*, I, 404–405.

24 *Cf.* Helmut Berve, "Miltiades. Studien zur Geschichte des Mannes und seiner Zeit," *Hermes. Zeitschrift für klassische Philologie. Einzelschriften*, Heft 2 (Berlin, 1937), 71–72.

25 Busolt, *Lakedaimonier*, I, 467.

26 *Cf.* Hermann Strasburger, "Der Einzelne und die Gemeinschaft im Denken der Griechen," *Historische Zeitschrift*, CLXXVII (1954), 228.

27 *Ibid.*, 240.

28 Herodotus, 1.152; 5.49–55.

29 Busolt, *Lakedaimonier*, I, 370–71. G. B. Grundy, *Thucydides and the History of His Age* (2 vols.; Oxford, 1948), I, 225ff., argues that Sparta's actions outside the Peloponnese were almost invariably geared to the Peloponnesian balance of power.

30 Herodotus, 7.139; 9.60.

31 *Cf.* Busolt, *Lakedaimonier*, I, 250–51.

32 Thuc., 1.58; 1.69; 1.71; 6.73; 6.88; 7.25; 8.96.

33 Thuc., 1.75. See also Herodotus, 7.161: "The command of the sea, if the Lacedaemonians do not wish it, belongs to us."

34 Thuc., 1.86.

35 Thuc., 1.68–71; 1.74; 3.13.

36 Claims to this effect were made at an early time by Themistocles in Sparta after the restoration of Athens' city walls had progressed sufficiently to permit such demonstration of independence, Thuc., 1.91. Similar claims were made by Pericles, Thuc., 1.140.5; 1.141.1, and later in the war by Athenian envoys, Thuc., 6.82. Eventually the Athenians made it quite clear that they would no longer recognize Sparta's *prostasia*, Thuc., 1.73.1.

37 Thuc., 1.90.

38 Eduard Meyer, *Geschichte des Altertums* (2nd ed.; 5 vols; Stuttgart and Berlin, 1915), III, 460ff.; 473ff.; hereinafter cited as Meyer, *Geschichte*.

39 See Busolt, *Lakedaimonier*, I, 250–51.

40 Thuc., 1.101.

41 Grundy, *Thucydides*, I, 212ff. There are several references in Thucydides, 1.77.6; 1.101; 1.118.2; 4.55.

42 *Cf.* Busolt, *Griechische Geschichte*, Vol. III, Pt. 1, pp. 116ff.; Hammond, *History*, 262.

43 *Cf.* Busolt, *Griechische Geschichte*, Vol. III, Pt. 1, pp. 113ff.; 243ff.; Hammond, *History*, 262.

44 *Cf.* Busolt, *Lakedaimonier*, I, 415ff.

45 *Cf. Ibid.*, I, 417.

46 Busolt, *Griechische Geschichte*, Vol. III, Pt. 1, p. 87.

47 Meyer, *Geschichte*, III, 514.

48 Thuc., 1.122.

49 *Cf.* Helmut Berve, *Griechische Geschichte* (2 vols.; Freiburg i.Br., 1931), II, 6.

50 For a discussion of the contrast between Athens and Sparta see John H. Finley, Jr., *Thucydides* (Cambridge, 1947), 300.

51 *Cf.* G. Glotz, *Histoire Grecque* (2 vols.; Paris, 1948), II, 123–24, 145; Hermann Bengtson, *Griechische Geschichte von den Anfängen bis in die römische Kaiserzeit* (3rd ed.; Munich, 1965), 191.

52 *Ibid.*, 192–93.

53 Erik Wolf, *Griechisches Rechtsdenken* (3 vols.; Frankfurt a.M., 1956), Vol. III, Pt. 2, pp. 98–100.

54 Thuc., 1.125.

55 Thuc., 2.12.

56 Thuc., 1.84.2.

57 Thuc., 1.68.

58 *Cf.* Busolt, *Griechische Geschichte*, II, 68.

59 Thuc., 1.2.

60 Grundy, *Thucydides*, I, 202.

61 Schachermeyr, "Geschichte der Hellenen bis 356," 161.

62 Herodotus, 7.139; 8.1; 8.3.

63 F. Jacoby, *Atthis. The Local Chronicles of Ancient Athens* (Oxford, 1949), 222.

64 *Cf.* Busolt, *Lakedaimonier*, I, 370–71.

65 Herodotus, 7.139.

66 *Cf.* Finley, *Thucydides*, 83.

67 Aristotle, *The Athenian Constitution*, 23.

68 *Cf.* Wilhelm Roscher, *Leben, Werk und Zeitalter des Thukydides* (Göttingen, 1842), 240.

69 *Cf.* Bengtson, *Griechische Geschichte*, 172.

70 *Cf.* Busolt, *Griechische Geschichte*, Vol. III, Pt. 1, p. 39.

71 The new Athenian self-assurance is clearly revealed in a statement which Thucydides attributes to the Athenian Euphemus at Camarina: "After the

Median War we had a fleet, and so got rid of the empire and supremacy of the Lacedaemonians," Thuc., 6.82.

72 This contention of Diodorus Siculus, 11.37.1–5, seems quite plausible.

73 Thuc., 1.96.

74 *Cf.* Busolt, *Griechische Geschichte,* Vol. III, Pt. 1, p. 68.

75 Thuc., 1.95.

76 *Cf.* B. D. Meritt, H. T. Wade-Gery, M. F. McGregor, *The Athenian Tribute Lists* (4 vols.; Cambridge and Princeton, 1939–53), III, 231–32.

77 Thuc., 1.96.1.

78 Bengtson, *Griechische Geschichte,* 186–87.

79 J. A. O. Larsen, "The Constitution and Original Purpose of the Delian League," 175.

80 *Cf.* Plutarch, *Themistocles,* 20.

81 *Cf.* J. A. O. Larsen, "The Constitution and Original Purpose of the Delian League," 211.

82 Busolt, *Griechische Geschichte,* Vol. III, Pt. 1, pp. 81–82.

83 *Ibid.,* 357–58. Many students have questioned the historicity of the Peace of Callias. For recent discussions of the controversy see R. Sealey, "The Peace of Callias Once More," *Historia. Zeitschrift für alte Geschichte,* III (1954–55), 325–33; J. H. Oliver, "The Peace of Callias and the Pontic Expedition of Pericles," *Historia,* VI (1957), 254–55; D. Stockton, "The Peace of Callias," *Historia,* VIII (1959), 61–73; A. Andrewes, "Thucydides and the Persians," *Historia,* X (1961), 15.

84 *Cf.* Bengtson, *Griechische Geschichte,* 188.

85 Glotz, *Histoire Grecque,* II, 189.

86 *Ibid.,* II, 192, 194.

87 Hans Schaefer, "Die attische Symmachie im zweiten Jahrzehnt ihres Bestehens," *Hermes. Zeitschrift für klassische Philologie,* LXXI (1936), 137; see also A. W. Gomme, *A Historical Commentary on Thucydides* (3 vols.; Oxford, 1945 and 1956), I, 335–36.

88 The subject of constitutional conformity will be taken up at greater length in Chapter 5.

89 *Cf.* Schachermeyr, "Geschichte der Hellenen bis 356," 170ff.

90 *Ibid.,* 166.

CHAPTER THREE

1 Thuc. 1.98.3; *cf.* G. Glotz, *Histoire Grecque* (2 vols.; Paris, 1948), II, 128.

2 Thuc., 1.98. The dates of the actions against both Euboea and Naxos are uncertain, see A. W. Gomme, *A Historical Commentary on Thucydides* (3 vols.; Oxford, 1945 and 1956), I, 398–99; hereinafter cited as Gomme, *Commentary.*

3 Thuc., 1.68–71.

4 Thuc., 1.76–77.

5 *Cf.* J. A. O. Larsen, "The Constitution and the Original Purpose of the Delian League," *Harvard Studies in Classical Philology,* LI (1940), 191, 207.

6 Thuc., 1.90.1; see also G. B. Grundy, *Thucydides and the History of His Age* (2 vols.; Oxford, 1948), I, 292.

7 *Cf.* Georg Busolt, *Griechische Geschichte bis zur Schlacht bei Chaeroneia* (3 vols.; Gotha, 1893–1904), Vol. III, Pt. 1 (1897), 298.

8 *Cf.* Glotz, *Histoire Grecque*, II, 145.

9 *Cf.* Busolt, *Griechische Geschichte*, Vol. III, Pt. 1, pp. 297ff., 322.

10 Glotz, *Histoire Grecque*, II, 150.

11 Thuc., 1.108. See also Hermann Bengtson, *Griechische Geschichte von den Anfängen bis in die römische Kaiserzeit* (3rd ed.; Munich, 1965), 204.

12 Bengtson, *Griechische Geschichte*, 204–205.

13 *Cf.* Eduard Meyer, *Geschichte des Altertums* (2nd ed.; 5 vols.; Stuttgart and Berlin, 1915), III, 593–97.

14 *Cf. Ibid.*, III, 604, 606.

15 *Cf. Ibid.*, III, 622.

16 B. D. Meritt, H. T. Wade-Gery, M. F. McGregor, *The Athenian Tribute Lists* (4 vols.; Cambridge and Princeton, 1939–53), III, 301; hereinafter cited as Meritt, *et al., ATL.*

17 *Cf.* Busolt, *Griechische Geschichte*, Vol. III, Pt. 1, pp. 345–46.

18 *Cf.* Hermann Wentker, *Sizilien und Athen—Die Begegnung der attischen Macht mit den Westgriechen* (Heidelberg, 1956), 84.

19 *Cf. Ibid.*, 85.

20 *Cf.* Herbert Nesselhauf, "Untersuchungen zur Geschichte der delisch-attischen Symmachie," *Klio. Beiträge zur alten Geschichte*, Beiheft XXX, N. F. Heft 17 (1933), 35.

21 *Cf.* Grundy, *Thucydides*, I, 197.

22 *Cf.* William Scott Ferguson, *Greek Imperialism* (Boston and New York, 1913), 39–40.

23 For the economic aspects of that control, see Grundy, *Thucydides*, I, 183ff.

24 *Cf.* Glotz, *Histoire Grecque*, II, 165; Busolt, *Griechische Geschichte*, Vol. III, Pt. 2 (1904), 758.

25 Thucydides does not mention the project; in fact the only source reference is Plutarch, *Pericles*, 17. However, the historicity of Pericles' proposal is generally accepted.

26 *Cf.* Glotz, *Histoire Grecque*, II, 165.

27 I have consulted for purposes of this analysis Nesselhauf, "Untersuchungen zur Geschichte der delisch-attischen Symmachie," 32–34; Meritt, *et al., ATL*, III, 279–80; Wentker, *Sizilien und Athen*, 88–89.

28 Thuc., 1.23.6; 1.88; 1.118.2.

29 Thuc., 2.61.

30 Thuc., 1.23.

31 Busolt, *Griechische Geschichte*, Vol. III, Pt. 2, pp. 758–59.

32 Grundy, *Thucydides*, I, 236.

33 Thuc., 1.140.

34 Thuc., 1.120.

35 See the charges of the Corinthians, Thuc. 1.124.

36 Thuc., 1.139.

37 Thuc., 1.75.3; 1.141; 6.83; 6.87.

38   Cf. Julius Beloch, *Griechische Geschichte* (4 vols.; Strassburg, 1893), I, 516.

39   Thuc., 1.75–76.

40   Thuc., 1.144.

41   Thuc., 2.18.

42   Cf. Grundy, *Thucydides*, I, 235.

43   Cf. Hans-Joachim Diesner, *Wirtschaft und Gesellschaft bei Thukydides* (Halle, 1956), 160.

44   Cf. Meyer, *Geschichte*, IV, 357–58.

45   Ferguson, *Greek Imperialism*, 22.

46   For Pericles' appraisal, see Thuc., 1.141–42; 2.13. The extent of Athenian financial resources is uncertain, but there is no question that they were considerable. See H. T. Wade-Gery and B. D. Meritt, "Athenian Resources in 449 and 431 B.C.," *Hesperia*, XXVI (1957), 163–97; and for a criticism of their thesis, see M. Chambers, "Studies on Thucydides, 1957–1962," *The Classical World*, LVII (1963), 19.

47   Meyer, *Geschichte*, IV, 340–41.

48   The advantages of naval over land forces are outlined as follows by Pseudo-Xenophon, *The Constitution of the Athenians*, II and III: they make it easy to hold allies in check and to intercept the imports of others; they can devastate the land of a stronger enemy; they can leave their home base; they produce extended supply lines; make possible by-passing of enemy territory; bring cultural enrichment, super-abundance of goods, and a diversified life; can inflict damage without suffering damage themselves; make the home territory invulnerable to enemy action because they enable their people to give up their country. See also Isocrates, *Panathenaicus*, 53.

49   Thuc., 1.143.4–5.

50   See the statement of the Spartan king Archidamus to the effect that the Athenians did not make themselves slaves of their soil, Thuc., 1.81.

51   Cf. Grundy, *Thucydides*, I, 448.

52   Thuc., 7.27.3, contends that the war of attrition launched from Decelea was a major cause of Athens' ruin. However, Agis, the Spartan king, complained that there was little point in a land siege through the occupation of Decelea unless Athens were cut off from the importation of grain by sea, Xenophon, *Hellenica*, 1.1.35.

53   See speech of the Mytilenians, Thuc., 3.13.

54   See Thuc., 7.36ff.; 7.55; 7.64; 7.86.

55   Cf. Meyer, *Geschichte*, IV, 550–51.

56   Thuc., 2.65.

57   Thuc., 7.42; 8.12.

58   Thuc., 7.12–14.

59   Thuc., 8.15.

60   Xenophon, *Hellenica*, 1.6.

61   That observation is made by the Mytilenian envoys, Thuc., 3.13.

62   Thuc., 1.82; 1.137; 2.7.

63   Thuc., 2.70.

64   Thuc., 3.35ff.

65 Thuc., 4.23; 4.48.
66 *Cf.* Meyer, *Geschichte*, IV, 394ff.
67 *Ibid.*, IV, 403.
68 Thuc., 5.25.
69 Thuc., 8, *passim*.
70 *Cf.* Glotz, *Histoire Grecque*, II, 733–34.
71 Xenophon, *Hellenica*, 1. and 2., *passim*.
72 *Ibid.*, 2.2.
73 Thuc., 5.13; 5.14.
74 Thuc., 2.61ff.
75 Thuc., 4.19.
76 Meyer, *Geschichte*, IV, 610.
77 *Ibid.*, IV, 652.
78 Thuc., 2.59.
79 Thuc., 5.22.
80 Thuc., 5.43; 5.46–47; 5.118.
81 Thuc., 6.10.2.
82 *Cf.* Busolt, *Griechische Geschichte*, Vol. III, Pt. 2, p. 1197.
83 *Cf.* Meyer, *Geschichte*, IV, 474, 481.
84 Thuc., 4.118.
85 *Cf.* Meyer, *Geschichte*, IV, 471.
86 Thuc., 6.76–81.
87 Thuc., 6.90.
88 *Cf.* Grundy, *Thucydides*, I, 74ff.; 91.
89 Thuc., 5.27.
90 *Cf.* Eduard Schwartz, *Das Geschichtswerk des Thukydides* (2nd ed.; Bonn, 1929), 50.
91 *Cf. Ibid.*, 48–54.
92 *Cf.* Meyer, *Geschichte*, IV, 478.
93 Thuc., 8.18.

CHAPTER FOUR

1 Thuc., 1.99.3; 2.13.2; 3.13.5ff.; 3.19; 3.39.8; 3.46.3; 6.83–84.
2 Thuc., 1.82.1.
3 Thuc., 4.85.
4 Thuc., 3.3.1.
5 Thuc., 4.117.
6 Thuc., 3.31.
7 Thuc., 5.14.
8 Thuc., 8.15.
9 Thuc., 8.3.
10 Thuc., 1.139.3.
11 *Cf.* A. W. Gomme, *A Historical Commentary on Thucydides* (3 vols.; Oxford, 1945 and 1956), I, 373; hereinafter cited as Gomme, *Commentary*.
12 *Cf.* H. T. Wade-Gery and B. D. Meritt, "Athenian Resources in 449 and 431 B.C.," *Hesperia*, XXVI (1957), 163–97.

13 Fritz Schachermeyr, "Geschichte der Hellenen bis 356," in Fritz Valjavec (ed.), *Historia Mundi* (10 vols.; Bern, 1954), III, 172.

14 Thuc., 3.11–12; 6.10–11.

15 William Scott Ferguson, *Greek Imperialism* (Boston and New York, 1913), 72–73.

16 Athenian citizenship was finally given to the Samians in 405–404 when Athens was at the point of despair after the defeat at Aegospotami. *Cf.* Gomme, *Commentary*, I, 240.

17 Thuc., 5.30.

18 J. A. O. Larsen, "The Constitution of the Peloponnesian League," *Classical Philology*, XXVIII (1933), 266ff.

19 Georg Busolt, *Griechische Staatskunde* (3rd ed., 2 vols.; Munich, 1920–26), II, 1324.

20 Thuc., 1.19; 2.9; 4.79ff.; 5.57; 8.3. For general discussions of Sparta's relations with its allies see A. H. M. Jones, *Athenian Democracy* (Oxford, 1957), 68–69; Victor Ehrenberg, *The Greek State* (New York, 1964), 116.

21 Thuc., 8.18; 8.37; 8.57. See also Heinrich Triepel, *Die Hegemonie. Ein Buch von führenden Staaten* (Stuttgart, 1938), 371; hereinafter cited as Triepel, *Hegemonie*.

22 Thuc., 1.87; 1.119; 1.125.

23 A detailed analysis of the proceedings is given in Triepel, *Hegemonie*, 370.

24 See *ibid.*, 371. For a detailed treatment consult Eduard Schwartz, *Das Geschichtswerk des Thukydides* (2nd ed.; Bonn, 1929), 46ff.; hereinafter cited as Schwartz, *Thukydides*.

25 J. A. O. Larsen, "The Constitution of the Peloponnesian League," 6–7.

26 See G. E. M. de Ste. Croix, "The Character of the Athenian Empire," *Historia. Zeitschrift für alte Geschichte*, III (1954), 20 n.5.

27 *Ibid.*, 20.

28 Thuc., 1.144.2.

29 *Cf.* Triepel, *Hegemonie*, 343–44.

30 *Cf.* G. B. Grundy, *Thucydides and the History of His Age* (2 vols.; Oxford, 1948), I, 202.

31 Herbert Nesselhauf, "Untersuchungen zur Geschichte der delisch-attischen Symmachie," *Klio. Beiträge zur alten Geschichte*, Beiheft XXX, N. F. Heft 17 (1933), 62–65.

32 *Cf.* Jacqueline de Romilly, *Thucydides and Athenian Imperialism* (transl. by Philip Thody, New York, 1963), 69–70; hereinafter cited as Romilly, *Athenian Imperialism*.

33 Nesselhauf, "Untersuchungen zur Geschichte der delisch-attischen Symmachie," 64–65.

34 See Romilly, *Athenian Imperialism*, 71ff.

35 F. Schachermeyr, "Geschichte der Hellenen bis 356," 171.

36 Thuc., 1.99.

37 For a lucid discussion of the various imperialist factions in Athens see Romilly, *Athenian Imperialism*, 60ff.

38 *Ibid.*, 61–62.

39 *Ibid.*, 65.

40 *Cf.* G. Glotz, *Histoire Grecque* (2 vols.; Paris, 1948), II, 146; Schwartz, *Thukydides,* 66ff.
41 Thuc., 1.103.
42 Eduard Meyer, *Geschichte des Altertums* (2nd ed.; 5 vols.; Stuttgart and Berlin, 1915), IV, 354.
43 *Ibid.,* 356.
44 Thuc., 5.22.
45 Victor Ehrenberg, *Aspects of the Ancient World* (New York, 1946), 88.
46 *Cf.* Gomme, *Commentary,* I, 384–85; Triepel, *Hegemonie,* 351.
47 *Cf.* Gomme, *Commentary,* I, 384–85.
48 *Ibid.,* I, 340.
49 Glotz, *Histoire Grecque,* II, 606.
50 *Cf.* Triepel, *Hegemonie,* 351ff.
51 Thuc., 1.120.1–2.
52 Thuc., 6.85.
53 F. Schachermeyr, "Geschichte der Hellenen bis 356," 171.
54 Julius Beloch, *Griechische Geschichte* (4 vols.; Strassburg, 1893), I, 498; T. J. Quinn, "Thucydides and the Unpopularity of the Athenian Empire," *Historia. Zeitschrift für alte Geschichte,* XIII (July, 1964), 257–66.
55 *Cf.* Quinn, "Thucydides and the Unpopularity of the Athenian Empire," 258–59.
56 See D. W. Bradeen, "The Popularity of the Athenian Empire," *Historia. Zeitschrift für alte Geschichte,* IX (1960), 257–69.
57 Thuc., 1.35.5; 4.60; 6.85.
58 Jones, *Athenian Democracy,* 69.
59 Glotz, *Histoire Grecque,* II, 157.
60 *Cf. Ibid.,* II, 626.
61 Thuc., 7.57.
62 Thuc., 6.87.
63 Thuc., 6.18.1–3; 7.63.
64 Gomme, *Commentary,* I, 335.
65 Thuc., 1.69–71.
66 Thuc., 5.21; 5.25; 5.27–29; 5.31; 5.47; 5.51; 5.57.
67 Thuc., 1.115; see also Gomme, *Commentary,* I, 351.
68 *Cf.* Nesselhauf, "Untersuchungen zur Geschichte der delisch-attischen Symmachie," 10. Nesselhauf's thesis has not been universally accepted; however, a recent study states essential agreement with Nesselhauf, Russell Meiggs, "The Crisis of Athenian Imperialism," *Harvard Studies in Classical Philology,* LXVII (1963), 9.
69 Thuc., 1.117.
70 Thuc., 2.72ff.
71 Thuc., 7.57.
72 Thuc., 7.58.
73 Georg Busolt, *Griechische Geschichte bis zur Schlacht bei Chaeroneia* (3 vols.; Gotha, 1893–1904), Vol. III, Pt. 2 (1904), 1119–20.
74 Thuc., 4.88.
75 Thuc., 4.60; 4.65.

76 Thuc., 1.58.1; 1.75.1; 3.113.6; 4.79; 4.82; 4.108.
77 Thuc., 3.2.
78 Meyer, *Geschichte*, IV, 355.
79 Thuc., 4.108.
80 Thuc., 4.131.
81 Thuc., 5.32.
82 Thuc., 8.24; 8.30; 8.32.
83 Thuc., 8.23; 8.32.
84 Thuc., 8.23.
85 Thuc. 8.62.
86 *Cf.* Schachermeyr, "Geschichte der Hellenen bis 356," 170.
87 *Cf.* Triepel, *Hegemonie*, 374.
88 Thuc., 1.96.1.
89 Aristotle, *The Athenian Constitution*, 23.2.
90 *Cf.* Werner Jaeger, *Paideia: The Ideals of Greek Culture* (2nd ed.; 3 vols.; New York, 1945), I, 410–11.
91 *Panathenaicus*, 403–405, 407, 411–13, 431; *Panegyricus*, 177ff., 183, 187, 195.
92 *Cf.* Ferguson, *Greek Imperialism*, 65–66.
93 For a lucid discussion of the Athenian predicament resulting from the impossibility of building an empire on the foundation of consent see Romilly, *Athenian Imperialism*, 315ff.
94 Thuc., 6.87. The same thought was expressed by Alcibiades, Thuc., 6.18.
95 Thuc., 2.11; 4.92; 5.69; 6.90.
96 Thuc., 3.42–48.
97 Thuc., 6.13.
98 Thuc., 1.144.1.
99 Thuc., 6.18; 6.90.
100 Thuc., 2.63.
101 Thuc., 2.65.
102 Thuc., 6.24.
103 *Cf.* Meyer, *Geschichte*, IV, 497–98; Thuc., 6.91.
104 Thuc., 7.33.
105 Thuc., 6.10–11.
106 Thuc., 7.28.
107 Thuc., 3.36–40.
108 Thuc., 2.63.2.
109 See Euphemus' speech to the people of Camarina, Thuc., 6.85.
110 B. D. Meritt, H. T. Wade-Gery, M. F. McGregor, *The Athenian Tribute Lists* (4 vols.; Cambridge and Princeton, 1939–53), III, 156.
111 Such is the contention of Plutarch, *Themistocles*, 20.
112 Thuc., 1.120.2.
113 Thuc., 1.1.
114 *Cf.* Meyer, *Geschichte*, IV, 366ff.
115 *Ibid.*, IV, 619.
116 Thuc., 3.91; 5.84–114.
117 Thuc., 2.8.

118 Meyer, *Geschichte*, IV, 357.
119 Thuc., 5.53.
120 Thuc., 2.72.
121 *Cf.* John H. Finley, Jr., *Thucydides* (Cambridge, 1947), 178.
122 Thuc., 3.2.
123 Thuc., 1.71.4.
124 Thuc., 1.75.4.
125 Thuc., 1.86.
126 Thuc., 1.35; 1.40.
127 Grundy, *Thucydides*, I, 356.
128 Thuc., 5.97.
129 The practical, political and the moral dilemma of neutrals was pointed to by Wilhelm Roscher, *Leben, Werk und Zeitalter des Thukydides* (Göttingen, 1842), 243, 491; hereinafter cited as Roscher, *Thukydides*.
130 *Ibid.*, 491.
131 Thuc., 3.82–84.
132 Roscher, *Thukydides*, 243–44.
133 Thuc., 4.87.
134 Thuc., 4.120.
135 Roscher, *Thukydides*, 243.
136 Thuc., 1.32.
137 Thuc., 2.72.
138 Thuc., 4.85.
139 Thuc., 6.80.
140 Thuc., 1.32.4; *cf.* Triepel, *Hegemonie*, 358.
141 *Cf.* Roscher, *Thukydides*, 491; Thuc., 3.82.
142 Thuc., 1.75.4.
143 Thuc., 5.29ff.
144 A. Andrewes, "Thucydides on the Causes of the War," *Classical Quarterly*, N.S., IX (November, 1959), 229.
145 Thuc., 5.57.

CHAPTER FIVE

1 Thuc., 3.82.
2 Thuc., 3.52.
3 Thuc., 8.71.
4 Thuc., 8.70–71.
5 Thuc., 8.90.
6 Thuc., 4.85.
7 Thuc., 4.20.
8 Thuc., 8.18; 8.37; 8.58.
9 *Cf.* Georg Busolt, *Die Lakedaimonier und ihre Bundesgenossen* (Leipzig, 1878), I, 306–307; hereinafter cited as Busolt, *Lakedaimonier*.
10 *Cf.* Eduard Meyer, *Geschichte des Altertums* (2nd ed.; 5 vols.; Stuttgart and Berlin, 1915), III, 479.
11 See Jacqueline de Romilly, *Thucydides and Athenian Imperialism* (transl. by Philip Thody, New York, 1963), 43–44.

12 Thuc., 7.68.

13 Thuc., 2.62.

14 Thuc., 6.18.4; 6.90.

15 Thuc., 6.15.

16 Thuc., 6.18.2–3.

17 For a detailed discussion of the sociological causes and effects of constitutional conformity the reader is referred to Heinrich Triepel, *Die Hegemonie. Ein Buch von führenden Staaten* (Stuttgart, 1938), 156ff.

18 *Cf.* Herodotus, 5.91.

19 Pseudo-Xenophon, *The Constitution of the Athenians*, 2.17.

20 Thuc., 1.82; 1.18–19.

21 Thuc., 6.76–80.

22 Thuc., 6.85.

23 Thuc., 4.86.

24 Thuc., 4.114.

25 Thuc., 4.120.

26 G. Glotz, *Histoire Grecque* (2 vols.; Paris, 1948), II, 606.

27 *Cf.* Plutarch, *Cimon*, 16.

28 *Cf.* Hans Schaefer, "Die attische Symmachie im zweiten Jahrzehnt ihres Bestehens," *Hermes. Zeitschrift für klassische Philologie*, LXXI (1936), 138.

29 *Cf.* Glotz, *Histoire Grecque*, II, 125.

30 *Cf.* Hermann Bengtson, *Griechische Geschichte von den Anfängen bis in die römische Kaiserzeit* (3rd ed.; Munich, 1965), 208.

31 The Athenian intercession in Miletus in 450–49 apparently was not designed to establish democracy. The date of the Milesian democracy is controversial, see John P. Barron, "Milesian Politics and Athenian Propaganda," *Journal of Hellenic Studies*, LXXXII (1962), 1–6.

32 Georg Busolt, *Griechische Staatskunde* (3rd ed.; 2 vols.; Munich, 1920–26), II, 1350; hereinafter cited as Busolt, *Staatskunde*. For a detailed analysis of Athenian actions in relation to subject cities see B. D. Meritt, H. T. Wade-Gery, M. F. McGregor, *The Athenian Tribute Lists* (4 vols.; Cambridge and Princeton, 1939–53), III, 149ff.

33 Pseudo-Xenophon, 3.10–11, gives a psychological explanation: Οἱ γὰρ ὅμοιοι τοῖς ὁμοίοις εὖνοί εἰσι, contending that the Athenians preferred the "worthless" people in towns where party conflicts were raging.

34 See G. Vlastos, "Isonomia," *American Journal of Philology*, LXXIV (1953), 350–51.

35 *Ibid.*, 356-57.

36 A good discussion of the problem is found in Meyer, *Geschichte*, III, 479.

37 Glotz, *Histoire Grecque*, II, 606.

38 Pseudo-Xenophon, 3.10–11; see comment by Hartvig Frisch, *The Constitution of the Athenians* (Copenhagen, 1942), 151.

39 Thuc., 1.102.

40 This is suggested in the speech of the Corinthian, Thuc., 1.122.1.

41 *Cf.* Georg Busolt, *Griechische Geschichte bis zur Schlacht bei Chaeroneia* (3 vols.; Gotha, 1893–1904), Vol. III, Pt. 2 (1904), 1251.

42 Busolt, *Lakedaimonier*, I, 133–34.

43 Thuc., 5.32.3.
44 Busolt, *Lakedaimonier*, I, 134–35.
45 Thuc., 5.31.
46 Thuc., 5.29.
47 Meyer, *Geschichte*, IV, 468.
48 *Ibid.*, IV, 470.
49 Busolt, *Griechiche Geschichte*, Vol. III, Pt. 1 (1897), 315ff.
50 Glotz, *Histoire Grecque*, II, 146.
51 Thuc., 4.78.
52 *Cf.* Glotz, *Histoire Grecque*, II, 161.
53 *Ibid.*, II, 163.
54 *Cf.* Meyer, *Geschichte*, III, 590.
55 *Ibid.*, IV, 348–49.
56 Thuc., 5.44.
57 Thuc., 5.82.
58 *Cf.* Meyer, *Geschichte*, IV, 624.
59 *Ibid.*, III, 590.
60 A. H. M. Jones, *Athenian Democracy* (Oxford, 1957), 67–69.
61 Thuc., 8.48.5; 8.64.5.
62 *Cf.* Julius Beloch, *Griechische Geschichte* (4 vols.; Strassburg, 1893), I, 498.
63 Thuc., 3.82.
64 *Cf.* Busolt, *Griechische Geschichte*, Vol. III, Pt. 2, 848.
65 Busolt, *Staatskunde*, II, 1313.
66 This in essence is the argument presented by D. W. Bradeen, "The Popularity of the Athenian Empire," *Historia. Zeitschrift für alte Geschichte*, IX (1960), 257–69, and T. J. Quinn, "Thucydides and the Unpopularity of the Athenian Empire," *Historia. Zeitschrift für alte Geschichte*, XIII (July, 1964), 257–66.

CHAPTER SIX

1 Thuc., 1.18.
2 Thuc., 1.84.3.
3 A. W. Gomme, *A Historical Commentary on Thucydides* (3 vols.; Oxford, 1945 and 1956), I, 128ff.; hereinafter cited as Gomme, *Commentary*.
4 *Ibid.*, I, 167.
5 Such is the charge made in the speech of the Athenian envoys at Sparta, Thuc., 1.77.6.
6 Thuc., 1.141ff.
7 Aristotle, *Politics*, 1270b, 1271a.
8 *Cf.* Hermann Strasburger, "Die Entdeckung der politischen Geschichte durch Thukydides," *Saekulum* (1955), 422.
9 Thuc., 1.101; 1.118.
10 Thuc., 1.76.1; 4.80.
11 Aristotle, *Politics*, 1271b.
12 Thuc., 1.68–69.
13 Thuc., 1.68ff.; 4.15–38; 8.96.

14 Thuc., 5.36.

15 Thuc., 1.94ff.; 1.128ff.

16 *Cf.* Georg Busolt, *Die Lakedaimonier und ihre Bundesgenossen* (Leipzig, 1878), I, 354–55; hereinafter cited as Busolt, *Lakedaimonier.*

17 *Cf.* Eduard Meyer, *Geschichte des Altertums* (2nd ed.; 5 vols.; Stuttgart and Berlin, 1915), IV, 637. Aristotle contends that much of the corruption in Sparta was traceable to its institutions, *Politics,* 1270b.

18 Thuc., 1.87; 5.13; 5.17.

19 Thuc., 5.36.

20 *Cf.* Busolt, *Lakedaimonier,* I, 7.

21 This is the contention of Plutarch, *Alcibiades,* 24.

22 Thuc., 1.2; 1.6.

23 *Cf.* Jacqueline de Romilly, *Thucydides and Athenian Imperialism* (transl. by Philip Thody, New York, 1963), 60ff.; hereinafter cited as Romilly, *Athenian Imperialism.*

24 Hartvig Frisch, *The Constitution of the Athenians* (Copenhagen, 1942), 66ff.

25 Helmut Berve, "Miltiades. Studien zur Geschichte des Mannes und seiner Zeit," *Hermes. Zeitschrift für klassische Philologie. Einzelschriften,* Heft 2 (1937), 88ff.; also Georg Busolt, *Griechische Geschichte bis zur Schlacht bei Chaeroneia* (3 vols.; Gotha, 1893–1904), Vol. III, Pt. 2 (1904), 819-21.

26 Such is the contention of Pseudo-Xenophon, *The Constitution of the Athenians,* 2.14.

27 Meyer, *Geschichte,* III, 558–64.

28 *Cf.* Frank Burr Marsh, *Modern Problems in the Ancient World* (Austin, 1943), 36.

29 See Aristophanes, *Peace.*

30 *Cf.* G. B. Grundy, *Thucydides and the History of His Age* (2 vols.; Oxford, 1948), I, 202.

31 *Cf.* Fritz Schachermeyr, "Geschichte der Hellenen bis 356," in Fritz Valjavec (ed.), *Historia Mundi* (10 vols.; Bern, 1954), III, 168.

32 David Grene, *Man in His Pride—A Study in the Political Philosophy of Thucydides and Plato* (Chicago, 1950), 36.

33 See also Herodotus, 5.78.

34 Thuc., 2.39–40.

35 Thuc., 2.39.

36 See speech of Athenagoras, Thuc., 6.39.

37 Thuc., 8.86.

38 Thuc., 1.138.

39 Thuc., 2.65.

40 Thuc., 2.59.

41 Thuc., 1.104.

42 Thuc., 6.24.

43 Thuc., 6.27–28.

44 Thuc., 2.65.

45 Thuc., 7.48.

46 Thuc., 3.98.5.

47 Thuc., 8.68.

48 Xenophon, *Hellenica*, 1.7.1–7.

49 *Cf*. Grundy, *Thucydides*, I, 219.

50 Thuc., 4.26; 4.80.

51 Meyer, *Geschichte*, IV, 609.

52 *Ibid*., IV, 629–30.

53 *Cf*. Grene, *Man in His Pride*, 48.

54 Meyer, *Geschichte*, III, 516.

55 *Ibid*., III, 571.

56 *Cf*. John H. Finley, Jr., *Thucydides* (Cambridge, 1947), 171ff.

57 *Cf*. Meyer, *Geschichte*, IV, 575.

58 Aristotle, *The Athenian Constitution*, 29.

59 Meyer, *Geschichte*, IV, 599.

60 *Cf*. C. Hignett, *A History of the Athenian Constitution to the End of the Fifth Century B.C.* (Oxford, 1952), 280.

61 Meyer, *Geschichte*, IV, 635.

62 *Ibid*., IV, 659–61.

63 Thuc., 3.82–84.

64 Meyer, *Geschichte*, IV, 629–30.

65 Fritz Schachermeyr, "Geschichte der Hellenen bis 356," 193.

66 *Cf*. Lionel Pearson, "Popular Ethics in the World of Thucydides," *Classical Philology*, LII (1957), 230.

67 Thuc., 3.37.

68 Evidence of this is to be found in Thuc., 2.18; 3.42; 6.13; 6.24.

69 Aristotle, *The Athenian Constitution*, 28.

70 Only once, Thucydides reports, did Alcibiades do his fatherland a great service when he prevented the Athenian army in Samos from sailing against their city, 8.86. Thucydides' judgment of Pericles perhaps was more idealistic than was warranted by the facts. Plato did not consider him the *spoudaios* as did Thucydides, see Gomme, *Commentary*, I, 65, 69.

71 *Cf*. Raphael Sealey, "The Entry of Pericles into History," *Hermes. Zeitschrift für klassische Philologie*, LXXXIV (1956), 234–47.

72 See Thuc., 2.53; 2.59–61; 3.37; 3.98; 4.28; 6.27; 6.53ff.; 7.48–49; 8.68.

73 Thuc., 2.65.

74 Thuc., 4.27–28.

75 Thuc., 2.64.

76 *Cf*. Hans Herter, "Pylos und Melos," *Rheinisches Museum für Philologie*, XCVII (1954), 322–24.

77 For the thoughts expressed in this paragraph I have relied largely on Hans Herter, "Pylos und Melos," *passim*.

78 The elusive meaning of the Melian Dialogue has produced an abundance of literature. Among the more recent discussions the following should be mentioned: Felix M. Wassermann, "The Melian Dialogue," *Transactions of the American Philological Association*, LXXVIII (1947), 18–26; Max Treu, "Athen und Melos und der Melierdialog des Thukydides," *Historia. Zeitschrift für alte Geschichte*, II (1953–54), 253–73; Walter Eberhardt, "Der Melierdialog und die Inschriften ATL/A9 (IG I²63+) IG²97+," *Historia. Zeitschrift für*

alte Geschichte, VIII (1959), 284–314; A. Andrewes, "The Melian Dialogue and Pericles' Last Speech," *Proceedings of the Cambridge Philological Society,* CLXXXVI (1960), 1–10.

79 *Cf.* Hans Herter, "Freiheit und Gebundenheit des Staatsmannes bei Thukydides," *Rheinisches Museum für Philologie,* XCIII (1950), 144–45.

CHAPTER SEVEN

1 John H. Finley, Jr., *Thucydides* (Cambridge, 1947), 20.

2 Thuc., 1.80–85.

3 Thuc., 1.69–71.

4 See Victor Ehrenberg, "Polypragmosyne: A Study in Greek Politics," *Journal of Hellenic Studies,* LXVII (1947), 53.

5 Thuc., 7.27.

6 *Cf.* Fritz Schachermeyr, *Griechische Geschichte* (Stuttgart, 1960), 202.

7 Thuc., 1.77.6.

INDEX